LIFE IN
ROMAN BRITAIN

Life in
ROMAN
BRITAIN

ANTHONY BIRLEY

English Life Series
Edited by PETER QUENNELL

LONDON: B. T. BATSFORD LTD
NEW YORK: G. P. PUTNAM'S SONS

First published 1964

Third impression 1968

© Anthony Birley, 1964

Made and printed in Great Britain
by William Clowes and Sons, Limited, London and Beccles
for the publishers
B. T. BATSFORD LTD
4 Fitzhardinge Street, Portman Square, London, W.1
G. P. PUTNAM'S SONS
200 Madison Avenue, New York, N.Y. 10016

Preface

Times have changed, for the better, since 1936 when R. G. Collingwood wrote in the bibliography of *Roman Britain and the English Settlements* that 'modern books wholly dealing with Roman Britain are not very numerous'. Indeed one now feels the need for some excuse for adding yet another general work on the same subject. The careful student will not find any great originality of treatment, but I have tried to consider each part of the subject afresh; and this book differs from others on the same subject, in that it is profusely illustrated. I have tried to choose some unfamiliar pictures as well as old favourites, and I have not hesitated to go to a Continental source if no British illustration is available, which I think is a legitimate procedure when dealing with one province of a great empire. I should perhaps also explain that the map on p. xvi is intended simply to show as many as possible of the places mentioned in the text, and is not a comprehensive map of Roman Britain.* For this readers may be referred to the Ordnance Survey Map of Roman Britain (3rd ed. 1956).

As well as my general debt to all the books and articles in specialist journals, I have particular debts to acknowledge, to my father, Professor Eric Birley, who initially encouraged me to undertake this book and has given me the benefit of his advice at every stage; to my friend and former tutor Mr C. E. Stevens, who taught me most of the Roman History I know; to my

---

*Complete consistency in the use of ancient and modern place-names has not been possible. One instance may cause confusion: I have preferred the form *Vriconium* to *Viroconium* for Wroxeter, perhaps perversely, as there is no space to argue it here.

friend, Dr J. J. Wilkes, who read most of my manuscript; to my friend Dr Graham Webster, who gave me valuable advice on the subject matter of Chapter V; and to my wife, who typed the manuscript and encouraged me throughout the writing of the book. Any errors that remain or have crept back in are my responsibility alone.

NOTE TO SECOND IMPRESSION

A reprinting has given me the opportunity to attend to some misprints, to remove a number of ambiguities of wording, and to correct one or two factual errors. I am grateful to friends and reviewers who have drawn my attention to some of these. Omissions and unevenness of treatment may remain : standard concepts of the pattern of rural occupation in Roman times, for example, may before long be altered radically. Much work is in progress. But it is perhaps too early for a new synthesis. Reviewers were kind enough to note and approve my reliance on epigraphic material. Now at last the monumental *Roman Inscriptions of Britain* (1965) has appeared, edited by the late R. G. Collingwood and Mr R. P. Wright. Most of the entries in sections I and II of my Index are there and readers will now be able to find for themselves the evidence for characters such as Q. Calpurnius Concessinius or Flavius Antigonus Papias, Julia Lucilla or Tadia Vallaunius.

NOTE TO THIRD IMPRESSION

In 1967 Sheppard Frere's *Britannia* appeared. It seems best to refer to it here: it replaces Collingwood as the standard work. Other new items have been added at the end of each chapter. With the publication of the C.B.A. Report on Rural Settlement (see p. 99) in 1966, much new material is now accessible, making obsolete some of my original chapter V. This I have emended as far as was possible. A few improvements have been made elsewhere.

A. R. B.

Contents

List of Illustrations

Note—Except where stated, all dates are A.D.

LIST OF ILLUSTRATIONS

xiii

Acknowledgment

The author and publishers wish to thank the following for the illustrations appearing in this book:
Aerofilms and Aero Pictorial Ltd for pages 16, 34, 52 and 72; the Ashmolean Museum, Oxford for pages 39, 56 and 129 (top); Institut Archéologique, Arlon for page 97; Bath City Corporation for page 150; Belgrade Museum for page 19; Bibliothèque Nationale, Paris for page 38; Bodleian Library, Oxford for page 167; the Trustees of the British Museum for pages 4, 7, 13, 14 (both), 21, 51, 54, 71 (top), 83, 111 (bottom), 113, 122, 125, 133, 153, 155, 156 (both), 157 (bottom), 158 (top), 159 (bottom), 164 and 169; Chester Corporation for page 124; the Trustees of Chesters Museum, near Hexham (photograph by J. E. Hedley) for pages 79, 103 and 148 (top); the late Brian Clayton for page 100; Colchester and Essex Museum, Colchester for pages 29, 60, 73 (bottom), 138, 157 (top) and 160; Corbridge Museum for page 137; Department of Archaeology, Durham University for pages 128 and 132; Photographie Giraudon for pages 114 and 115; City of Gloucester Museums for page 36; Hunterian Museum, Glasgow for page 148; Kent County Council for page 90; A. F. Kersting, f.r.p.s. for page 70; Kingston upon Hull Museums for page 101; Langres Museum for page 131; City of Lincoln Corporation for pages 69 and 73 (top); City of London Corporation for page 143; London Museum for pages 62–3, 75 and 142; Altertumsmuseum, Mainz for pages 82, 95 and 105; Mansell Collection for pages 2, 8, 25, 28, 32–3, 35, 37, 46, 48, 49, 50, 53, 55, 64, 65, 80, 94, 104, 106, 107 (both), 109, 118–19, 129 (bottom), 135 and 139; Ministry of Public Building and Works for the frontispiece and pages 11,

ACKNOWLEDGMENT

42, 43, 44, 76, 88–9, 103, 127, 141 (top), 145, 163 and 168;
National Museum of Antiquities of Scotland, Edinburgh for pages
40 and 149; National Museum of Wales for pages 10, 45 and 71
(bottom); National Trust for page 147; Museum of Antiquities,
Newcastle upon Tyne for pages 141, 146, 158 (bottom) and
159; His Grace the Duke of Northumberland for page 51; *Radio
Times* Hulton Picture Library for pages 111 (top) and 112;
Royal Commission on Historical Monuments (England) for
pages 108, 117 and 144; St Albans City Council for page 102;
Dr J. K. St Joseph for pages 5, 6, 31, 58 and 166; Sarajevo
Museum for page 141 (bottom); Alan Sorrell for frontispiece
and pages 43, 62–3 and 88–9; Roman Fort and Museum, South
Shields for pages 110 and 134; Landesmuseum, Trier for pages
68, 85, 87, 98, 116 and 126; the Trustees of the Victoria and
Albert Museum for page 23; Kunsthistorisches Museum,
Vienna for page 9; Water Newton Excavation Committee for
page 130.

The jacket illustration is reproduced from a coloured en-
graving in Thomas Morgan, *Romano-British Mosaic Pavements.*

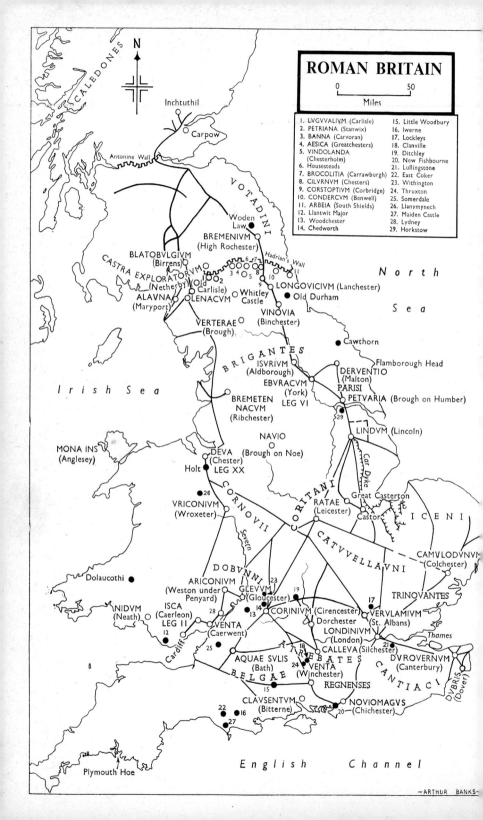

ROMAN BRITAIN

0   50

Miles

1. LVGVVALIVM (Carlisle)
2. PETRIANA (Stanwix)
3. BANNA (Carvoran)
4. AESICA (Greatchesters)
5. VINDOLANDA (Chesterholm)
6. Housesteads
7. BROCOLITIA (Carrawburgh)
8. CILVRNVM (Chesters)
9. CORSTOPTIVM (Corbridge)
10. CONDERCVM (Benwell)
11. ARBEIA (South Shields)
12. Llantwit Major
13. Woodchester
14. Chedworth

15. Little Woodbury
16. Iwerne
17. Lockleys
18. Clanville
19. Ditchley
20. New Fishbourne
21. Lullingstone
22. East Coker
23. Withington
24. Thruxton
25. Somerdale
26. Llanymynech
27. Maiden Castle
28. Lydney
29. Horkstow

~ARTHUR BANKS~

I

Britain at the Conquest

The first Roman emperor Augustus, it was generally agreed at the time of his death in A.D. 14, could be reasonably regarded as having extended the empire to its natural limits: 'the sea, the ocean and long rivers surround it; the legions, provinces and fleets are all mutually interconnected.' Augustus certainly left Rome the advice that 'the empire should be kept within these boundaries'. His advice was sound. He himself had brought to completion most of the achievements of his predecessors. Some of the grandiose plans of conquest formed by his assassinated great-uncle, the dictator Julius Caesar, had been abandoned: the Dacians north of the lower Danube had been brought to heel but not annexed; the Parthian empire had not been attacked, but the Romans had obtained peace with honour when the legionary eagles lost with Crassus had been returned; and the Germans beyond the Rhine and Danube had been left to their undisciplined savagery when the disaster of A.D. 9 had been at least partly avenged.

Caesar had invaded Britain twice, in 55 and 54 B.C. Augustus was tempted to complete the conquest:

> *Augustus will be regarded as a god on earth*
> *When the Britons are added to the empire,*

wrote the court poet Horace. But in his mature political wisdom Augustus preferred to let well alone.

Caesar's invasion of Britain had been a sensation at Rome, and the occasion for 20 days' public holiday. The island had

Julius Caesar

been known of in the Mediterranean for 500 years at least, but some of Cicero's acquaintance were still inclined to doubt its existence. Besides, the invasion involved the crossing of a tidal sea, to which the Romans were quite unused. Rome's ancient rival Carthage had once monopolised the sea trade in tin from Cornwall, a metal vital for the making of bronze. Rome's ally *Massilia* (Marseilles), a Greek colonial city, traded overland with Britain through middlemen on the Gulf of Finisterre. In 118 B.C. Rome founded a colony at Narbonne—the first official colony outside Italy—to wrest control of this trade route from *Massilia*. For the Romans were interested in metals, a fact which had reached the ears of Judas Maccabeus in far off Palestine: 'Now Judas had heard of the fame of the Romans . . . and what they had done in the country of Spain, for the winning of the mines of the silver and the gold which is there.' The colony at Narbonne was the first of many overseas colonies, so that it was in a sense in 118 B.C. that Britain first, if only indirectly, affected the course of European history.

Sixty years later, Julius Caesar, then the ambitious proconsul of Gaul, was to open the series of campaigns which brought the whole territory between the Mediterranean and the Rhine under Roman rule. In doing so, he twice invaded Britain, claiming in his memoirs, the *de bello Gallico*, where his motives are carefully disguised, that 'the people of Britain had assisted the Gauls in all their wars against Rome.' His invasions brought Britain directly to the attention of Rome for the first time.

Whatever the truth of Caesar's accusation, the island was certainly inhabited by people closely related to the Gauls of the mainland. He called them *Britanni*, and the island *Britannia*, evidently confusing the more correct form *Pretani* used by the

Greek explorer Pytheas with a name he knew in Gaul. The majority of the inhabitants of Britain were by this time Celtic, like the Gauls. They were thus part of a powerful nation called variously *Keltoi*, *Celtae*, *Galatae* and *Galli* by the inhabitants of the Mediterranean basin. Not a unified nation in the modern sense, the Celts were a people composed of tribes of varying size, usually politically independent of one another, with certain common characteristics, which had first become apparent in the area north of the Alps at the beginning of the sixth century B.C. It was there at this time that the iron-using warrior chieftains centred on Hallstatt in Austria first gained power, and from this base they expanded west, east and south, as far east as Asia Minor, where they gave their name to Galatia, and in the west to Spain and Britain. They plundered Greece and Italy also, and in 390 B.C. a group of them, returning from a raid in central Italy, captured Rome and held it to ransom.

The Mediterranean peoples saw in them at once a people different from themselves, taller and more powerfully built, fairer in skin and hair (their blondness accentuated by their custom of washing their hair in lime), blue-eyed, and differently dressed, wearing trousers and tunic. They were certainly taller than the average Roman, and more warlike also. The lure of the rich Greek and Etruscan civilisation in Italy was a powerful magnet for a people fond of personal adornment, such as gold torcs. After 390 B.C., nearly two centuries had to pass before the Romans were able to master the Celts settled in northern Italy; and the remainder of the Continental Celts, in Gaul, were not defeated until the campaigns of Julius Caesar.

The Celts of Britain were immigrants sprung from the Continental Celts. For centuries, ever since the formation of the island in fact, Britain had been a haven for refugees of all kinds. It required a little spirit to cross the North Sea or the Channel, but it was a short journey, and southern and eastern England is particularly easy to enter. The island is naturally divided into two by a line running from Flamborough Head in Yorkshire to Plymouth Hoe. North and west of this line, marked geologically by the Jurassic Ridge, are found all the real mountains of Britain, and the hard rock formations. South and east of it, the

Iron Age helmet from the Thames

country is more level and the river valleys, especially the Thames, and the ridgeways encourage penetration inland. Invaders equipped with improved industrial, agricultural and military techniques learned on the Continent found it a relatively easy matter to establish themselves against opposition from a native population without these advantages and with no assistance from the terrain. By contrast, in the highland zone the hillmen of Wales, the Pennines and the Highlands of Scotland were more difficult to dislodge, and in any case their lands were not so greatly sought after.

From about 600 B.C. the invaders brought with them to Britain the use of iron, giving them an immense advantage against the bronze-using natives. They were clearly Celts coming from the Low Countries and northern France. By the fourth century B.C. 'Albion' had become the land of the Pretani, which is apparently a Celtic name, to a visitor such as Pytheas. In the meantime new movements were taking place on the Continent, and in the mid third century a new wave of invaders, known as Marnians from their probable place of origin, began to colonise the south coast, the Yorkshire Wolds and perhaps even south-west Scotland. Finally, some 20 years before Caesar, the third and most advanced group of all, the Belgae, began to arrive. The Belgae, in Gaul and Britain alike, proved Caesar's most powerful enemies. In Britain their most aggressive tribe was based in Hertfordshire, but was already beginning to expand from there.

The evidence of archaeology and the descriptions of Caesar and other writers have combined to give us a fairly detailed picture of the character of the people of Britain at the moment

4

when they first made contact with Rome. They shared with other Celtic peoples a common language and religion and their material culture was generally only a little less advanced than that of the Continent. In practically every respect Britain was a cultural appendage of Gaul. Three features distinguished them from more primitive peoples such as the Germans. The first was their capacity to build hill-forts. The fortifying of hill tops with elaborate defences began in the third century B.C., probably as a measure of defence against the second wave of invaders. To construct the defences of a hill-fort like that at Cissbury Rings, it was necessary to shift 60,000 tons of chalk and to cut and put into position 10,000 15-foot posts to support the rampart, which indicates a high degree of engineering skill and political organisation. By the end of the second century they had begun to mint their own coinage, which indicates a developed trading activity and a certain degree of technological skill. Previously currency bars of iron had been in use. Thirdly, the Celts had become agriculturists, practising a settled farming economy. At first they farmed only the lighter, upland soils since their ploughs could do little more than scratch the surface. Because of this

Cissbury Rings, Sussex: an Iron Age hill-fort, enclosing 60 acres

Celtic agriculture : field-system at Smacam Down, Dorset

their commonest field size was a small rectangle less than 400 feet square which had to be ploughed and cross-ploughed many times. The square patchwork pattern of Celtic fields is still observable in many parts of the country. The Greek writer Diodorus quotes from Pytheas, who drew attention to their underground pits, which excavation has shown to be storage silos in which they kept roasted grain.

The Belgae brought with them a heavier plough, the *caruca*, fitted with coulter and ground-wrest, which could turn a real sod of earth. Thus the heavier soils of the valleys could be exploited for the first time, and it became profitable to cultivate the land in longer fields. When Caesar began his conquest of Gaul, further groups of immigrants crossed over as refugees, and the earlier inhabitants in the south reoccupied the hill-forts and extended their defences. A notable example is Maiden Castle where the ramparts and ditches were perhaps enlarged at this time, apparently to cope with the attacks of sling-using peoples.

Caesar's campaigns were inspired largely by his own political ends, to gain him popularity and prestige at Rome, and more important, to extend his military command for another five years, giving him time to build up a commanding position *vis-à-vis* his rivals. In this he succeeded, and the army with which he conquered Gaul and invaded Britain made him sole ruler of the Roman world. In Britain his chief opposition came from Cassivellaunus, leader of a Belgic tribe, the Catuvellauni. In his second campaign Caesar successfully stormed the stronghold of the Catuvellauni, probably the enormous earthwork at Wheathampstead in Hertfordshire. He exacted a formal tribute from the Britons, and forbade further expansion by the Catuvellauni. For a time the tribute may have been paid and the embargo on expansion heeded, but before long the Catuvellauni had transferred their mint and presumably their tribal centre from Hertfordshire to *Camulodunum* (Colchester), conquering the Trinovantes of Essex. Shortly after Caesar's invasion new immigrants had arrived in Britain led by one of Caesar's leading opponents in Gaul, Commius of the Atrebates, who established himself in Hampshire and Sussex. Caesar's heir Augustus somehow appears to have persuaded the heirs of Commius to adopt a philo-Roman policy as a counterbalance to the ambitions of the leader of the Catuvellauni, Cunobelinus, Shakespeare's 'radiant Cymbeline'. The coinage of these British chiefs, or kings, reflects their different policies. That of the Atrebates closely copies Roman originals, and bears the Latin word REX, a sign that the Atrebates knew some Latin, for the title of *rex* was anathema to the Romans, but was granted to allies of the Roman people. One coin issued by the Catuvellauni, by contrast, bears the Celtic word RICON, meaning 'king' like *rex*, but by its choice of language indicating independence of Rome. Likewise, the Catuvellaunian coinage was designed in spirited artistic independence of Roman coinage. One difference between the two British coinages is particularly striking: that of Cymbeline carries an ear of barley and that of the heirs of Commius a vine leaf, as if the one was proclaiming 'British beer is best',

Coins of the Atrebates and Catuvellauni

and the other was extolling wine imported from the Roman world.

Despite Roman pressure, Cymbeline's kingdom continued to expand, until most of the lowland zone of the country was in his hands or under his influence. Shortly after he died, his sons Caratacus and Togodumnus managed to evict the ruler of the Commian kingdom, Verica, who fled to Rome, asking for protection and redress as earlier British princes had done under Augustus and Caligula. This provided a convenient pretext for the Emperor Claudius to invade. His unbalanced predecessor, his nephew Caligula, had already, despite the advice of Augustus, planned to invade Britain, but called the expedition off at the last moment, contenting himself with building a large lighthouse at Boulogne. Claudius was desperately in need of military prestige and popularity, and the invasion of Britain provided an ideal opportunity. An expeditionary force was prepared in A.D. 43 of which the basis was formed by four legions, commanded by the experienced senatorial general Aulus Plautius, a relative of the Emperor's first wife. In spite of a

Invasion: soldiers preparing to leap ashore

mutiny at the embarkation port of Boulogne by soldiers who complained that Britain was 'another world', the crossing of the Channel and landing of the invasion army was successfully accomplished and the campaign was over with startling speed. In spite of active resistance, the Britons were no match for the disciplined Roman army in pitched battle. Togodumnus was killed and Caratacus fled to the west. Plautius called a halt when victory was in sight and sent for Claudius to allow him to receive in person the surrender of eleven British kings, perhaps even one from far off Orkney. Claudius returned home after sixteen days in Britain to celebrate a triumph. He renamed his son, born in 41, 'Britannicus'.

Claudius triumphing over the Britons

The Britons by the time of the conquest by Rome were not the equals of their conquerors in civilisation, but they were not the woad-painted savages of popular imagination. In the highland zone, a primitive pastoral economy, in which cattle were the measure of wealth, was still practised. But in the lowland zone a settled mixed farming economy was the rule. The Celtic farmers lived in timber-built farmsteads, mostly round in plan. The Catuvellauni at least were sufficiently powerful to dispense with the protection of hill-forts, except on their borders. The new capital of Cymbeline at *Camulodunum* was in the flat land of Essex at the mouth of the river Colne, strategically placed for trade with the Rhineland. It was hardly a town, but a collection of huts scattered over an area of several hundred acres, enclosed by a system of dyke defences. To a large extent they were self-sufficient, but the richer among them had grown accustomed to use, increasingly, imported tablewares from the Roman empire. In spite of any political implications behind the ear or barley on the Catuvellaunian coinage, wine was imported in

9

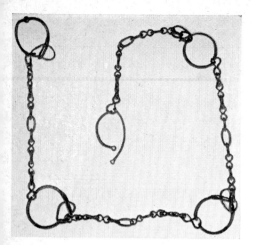

Slave chain from Llyn Cerrig Bach, Anglesey

considerable quantities by southern Britons of both pro-Roman and anti-Roman sympathies. They exported to pay for their luxuries. Not only corn, cattle, hides and iron went across the Channel, but gold and silver, which Cymbeline's kingdom did not possess, and must have acquired from the west and north by exchange or conquest. Hunting dogs may have been bred for export, but the slaves which the geographer Strabo, writing at the beginning of the first century A.D., lists, in addition to the other British exports mentioned, were certainly the fruits of conquest. Gang chains for slaves, an unpleasant reminder of the background to the rule of 'the radiant Cymbeline', have been found in several places from deposits of the pre-Roman period, including one from Llyn Cerrig Bach on Anglesey to which it may have come as a religious dedication to a shrine administered by the Celtic priesthood, the Druids. It is interesting that Strabo omits tin from the list. The reason was that the alternative source of supply in north-west Spain was now so firmly under Roman control that the Cornish mines had lost their markets.

Strabo, after discussing trade with Britain, commented that it would not be profitable for the Romans to make a province of the island, since the revenue from taxes would hardly pay for the garrison which he estimated would require one legion and some auxiliary regiments. As it was, excise duty on trade between Britain and the Continent was quite profitable enough. Strabo no doubt echoed official policy. Britain had been technically conquered by Caesar; all that was necessary was a formal annexation, but this was deferred, following the declared policy of Augustus. Even 100 years after the conquest by Claudius, the historian Appian wrote that Britain cost the Romans more than it gained them. The advisers of Claudius may have miscalculated (they were certainly misled as to the value of pearls from British

10

oysters). But the governing factor was prestige and ambition. The army mutinied at Boulogne because they were being led into another world: Britain was a kind of El Dorado until it was conquered.

Further Reading

M. Dillon and N. Chadwick, *The Celtic Realms*, 1967
D. R. Dudley and G. Webster, *The Rebellion of Boudicca*, 1962
—————, *The Roman Conquest of Britain*, 1965
C. Fox, *The Personality of Britain* (4th ed.), 1944
Ordnance Survey Map of Southern Britain in the Iron Age, 1962
T. G. E. Powell, *The Celts* (2nd ed.), 1959
A. L. F. Rivet, *Town and Country in Roman Britain* (2nd ed.) 1965: Chapter Two, 'The Celtic Background'
C. E. Stevens, 'Britain between the Invasions (54 B.C.–A.D. 43)' in W. F. Grimes (ed.), *Aspects of Archaeology in Britain and Beyond*, 1951

A Roman warship

II

Administration

With its formal annexation, Britain at once fell under the provisions of Roman Law. The writ of the *Lex Iulia de vi publica*
(the Julian Law concerning the public use of force), for
example, ran throughout the province, making it a capital
offence to bear arms without imperial authority. For 367 years
the civilian inhabitants were bound by this law, until they were
specifically exempted from it in 410 by the Emperor Honorius,
who instructed them to take up arms to defend themselves
against the invading Saxons, Scots and Picts after the garrison
had been withdrawn.

When the Emperor Claudius prepared to leave, after his
token participation in the successful invasion campaign, he gave
instructions to Aulus Plautius and his colleagues, 'to conquer
the rest'. If this meant the rest of the island, as it may have, his
orders were never carried out. Plautius rapidly overran the
lowland zone. Certain enclaves were left under the direct control
of their native princes, one of whom, Cogidubnus, the successor
to the pro-Roman peoples of Berkshire and Sussex, was made a
Roman citizen by Claudius and later, it would seem, a Roman
senator. Bearing the first two names of his patron the Emperor,
he was able to be styled 'Tiberius Claudius Cogidubnus, King
and Imperial Deputy in Britain' in a dedication he authorised a
guild of artisans to set up to Neptune and Minerva 'in honour
of the divine house' of the Emperor. But the treaties which
allowed Cogidubnus and his fellow client-princes their independence were subject to revision at their deaths.

12

Another tribe which had also clearly favoured Rome from the start in resentment at the expansionist policy of the house of Cymbeline, the Iceni of East Anglia, were also left in independence. The paramount chief of the vast, loosely-knit confederation of the Brigantes which covered all the Pennines, was similarly left outside the province. Other tribes beyond the boundary of the province made treaties with Rome. At the very opening of the invasion campaign, a chieftain of the Orkneys appears to have submitted

Claudius, Emperor 41–54

to Claudius, presumably at Colchester. In later periods peoples beyond the frontier were either in a treaty relationship, or in permanent hostility to Rome. Further annexations under later governors extended the boundaries of the province until it included the whole of England and Wales and much of Scotland. But the far north was finally abandoned in 211, and in its final form the province's only land frontier was Hadrian's Wall. At about this time the province was divided for administrative purposes into two and later, in the fourth century, into four and finally five 'provinces of the Britains'.

The personality of the province's conqueror had some importance. Claudius, for all his personal failings, which made him a laughing stock to the aristocracy of Rome, was a liberal-minded and progressive emperor, and he clearly intended that Britain should gain benefits from its accession to the empire. The philosopher and senator Seneca, who was himself alleged to have invested profitably in loans at exorbitant interest to ill-advised Britons, and by calling them in suddenly to have helped to provoke a rebellion (that of Boudicca), accused Claudius in a satirical pamphlet published after the latter's death, of a scandalous intention to make all the Britons Roman citizens, wanting 'to see everybody, Greek, Gauls, Spaniards, Britons, wearing togas'. The intention if it existed was probably not a serious one, but the story would only have had point if there was some substance in it. Claudius clearly favoured the Britons and

Septimius Severus, Emperor 193–211

no doubt others besides Cogidubnus gained citizenship and similar benefits from the emperor.

Personal visits paid to Britain by particular emperors had noticeable effects. Hadrian, during his visit in 122, not only ordered the construction of the frontier wall, the remains of which now bear his name, but greatly stimulated the economy of the province by encouraging public building. The life of the urban communities all over the province flourished as never before in the period after his visit. Severus came over in 208, and remained till his death at York in 211, with his family, court and a vast retinue. He too gave an impetus to public building, and it was probably he who ordered the construction of town walls for places such as Wroxeter, Caerwent and Aldborough. In the third century Britain was for a number of years ruled by separatist Gallic emperors, and latterly by 'Emperors of Britain'—Carausius and Allectus. Under their rule naturally more attention was paid to Britain than had been paid by the central government in Rome. But when Constantius recovered the island for the central government in 296, he made York his seat of residence as junior western emperor for a number of years, and in fact died there in 306. His presence in the island greatly stimulated the economy also, and may be the origin of Britain's surprising prosperity in the fourth century.

Constantius Chlorus, junior emperor 293–305, senior emperor 305–6

For the most part, however, the emperor remained a distant figure, revered as a god on earth, but never seen by the Britons in the flesh, and the character and policies of most emperors did not generally greatly affect the daily life of the provincials. 'Even bad emperors', as a Roman governor pointed out to an assembly of rebellious Gauls in 70, 'vent their spleen against those closest at hand'—the aristocracy and officialdom of the capital. But the emperors or their advisers were responsible for the selection of governors and of procurators (as the imperial receivers general of taxes and controllers of provincial finances were called). Until the fourth century the government of the province and the command in chief of its armed forces were exercised by the same man, as emperor's deputy, *legatus Augusti pro praetore*. The emperor, by a legal fiction originally designed to disguise his absolute rule, was technically appointed, by the senate and people of Rome, as *proconsul* of most of the provinces of the Empire, except those peaceful provinces with a high standard of living which did not require a strong military garrison. He himself directly appointed deputies, either senators of varying rank, or men from the next grade in the hierarchy of Roman public life, the *equites*. The governor of Britain was always chosen from the highest rank of senators, the former consuls, and among the provinces governed by former consuls, Britain was one of the two senior appointments, for its first two centuries as a Roman province. Thus the governors were usually men of high calibre.

In the fourth century, Britain, like the other provinces of the empire, was administered on a new basis. The civil and military powers were divided, the civil governor now being called the Vicar of Britain, and the military power being under the Duke of Britain; and later, as the danger from overseas increased, another high officer, the Count of the Saxon Shore, commanded the garrisons on the east coast.

The names and careers of many of the governors are known to us. The best known of all is Gnaeus Julius Agricola (governor, 78–84) naturally enough, for his son-in-law Tacitus wrote his biography. Ironically, Agricola was not a typical governor of Britain. He was, undoubtedly, a good choice by an emperor (Vespasian) who had himself participated in the conquest. He was of Celtic origin, from Fréjus in Provence, and he had served twice before in Britain as military tribune of a legion as a young man, and as commander of the Twentieth Legion in his

15

early 30s'. He came to Britain straight from
the ancient magistracy of the consulship at the
age of 37. But it was rare for Roman senators
to spend even two periods of their military
service in the same province. To spend three,
as Agricola did, was unique. It was commoner
practice to gain experience with the armies of
different provinces. Again, it was not common
for a governor of Britain to come there straight
from the consulship. Finally, Agricola served
seven years as governor, an exceptionally long
term. Only with these reservations in mind,
may the career of Agricola be regarded as a
reasonably typical case, for he served in the
normal mixture of civilian and military posts.
Tacitus described his service as governor in
glowing terms, no doubt with justification. The
governor was the supreme civil, military and
judicial authority. He was the penultimate court
of appeal (after him there was only the
emperor). Like many governors of Britain,
Agricola spent most of the summer each year
on campaign in the field. The winter months
were spent in supervising the affairs of the
civilian zone: road-building and maintenance,
the supervision of the public post, administration
of justice—hearing of law-suits and settling
disputes. Only the governor was entitled to
pronounce capital punishment. According to
Tacitus, Agricola on his arrival as governor,
after a brief punitive campaign in Wales, turned
his attention in his first winter to regulating
civilian matters, taking particular attention 'to
make the collection of taxes and tribute in
kind (food and fodder for the army) more
equitable'. In his second winter he made a
particular point of encouraging the erection of
public buildings and the education in the liberal

16

Part of the Fosse Way

arts of the sons of leading Britons. 'The result', Tacitus sardonically comments, 'was to create a fashion for porticoes, baths and
elegant banquets, which the ignorant provincials called civilisation, when it was in fact part of their servitude.' A matter of
particular importance for all governors was the maintenance and
extension of the road system. Aulus Plautius and his first successors had covered southern Britain with a network of roads,
and later governors had to keep them in good condition, providing teams of surveyors and foremen and organising levies
to provide labour if the army could not provide labour itself.

Most of the governors whose names and careers we know in
any detail can be seen to have been chosen well, for their special
qualifications. Q. Veranius and C. Suetonius Paulinus, for instance, had neither of them served in Britain before, but both
had had experience of mountain warfare, in the Taurus and
Atlas mountains respectively, and hence were the right men to
appoint for the subjugation of the Welsh mountains. Some
clearly owed their high office to their friendship with the
emperor. A. Platorius Nepos, for instance, was from the same
part of Spain as the Emperor Hadrian. His early career did not
indicate special promise. Roman senators were obviously
graded at the very outset of their careers, in their late teens, and
the men of non-aristocratic background who needed to serve as
military governors to ennoble themselves, had far greater
chance of high office if they started in one of the favoured posts.
Platorius Nepos began as a police commissioner of Rome, a
post which did not normally lead, ultimately, to a high command. But the accession of his friend Hadrian to the throne,
after Nepos had risen, slowly, to be governor of Thrace,
changed the situation for him. He was made consul, and then
governor of Lower Germany—the military zone of the Lower
Rhine. This post was one which very frequently led to the
command in Britain, in the hierarchy of promotion, and Hadrian
duly gave him this appointment. His *cursus*, as the official career
was called, engraved on a marble monument in his honour by
the citizens of the prosperous north-Italian port of Aquileia
when the news of his appointment was announced, gives his
full names and the details of his career (although the zealous

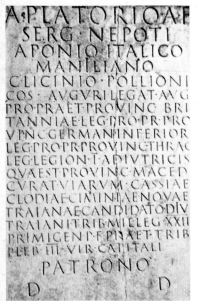

A·PLATORIO·A·
SERG·NEPOTI
APONIO·ITALICO
MANILIANO
CLICINIO·POLLIONI
COS·AVGVRILEGAT·AVG
PROPRAETPROVINC·BRI
TANNIAELEGIIROPR·PRO
VINCGERMANINFERIOR
LEGPROPRPROVINCTHRAC
LEGLEGIONTADIVTRICIS
QVAESTPROVINCMACED
CVRATVIARVM·CASSIAE
CLODIAECIMININAENOVAE
TRAIANAECANDIDATODIV
TRAIANITRIBMILLEGXXII
PRIMIGENPFPIAAETTRIB
PLEBIII·VIRCAPITALI
PATRONO
D   D

Inscription to the governor Nepos

Aquileians put some of his offices in the wrong sequence).

As governor of Britain, Nepos is named on a number of inscriptions from Hadrian's Wall recording building. The commonest record of the presence and activities of governors in Britain is the presence of their names on official inscriptions, sometimes purely honorific, recording that by their authority an inscription was set up in honour of the emperor, sometimes recording that the emperor through their agency had ordered the erection of a public building or a milestone.

The governor had a large staff to assist him in his duties, many of whom he was entitled to appoint personally. Chance has preserved details of letters asking governors to take people on their staff. The senator Pliny wrote to Neratius Marcellus, the governor of Britain, asking him to provide a post as military tribune for his friend Suetonius. In the event, Suetonius seems to have had second thoughts and resigned the appointment without taking it up. Another interesting case is a letter, preserved on a stone inscription, from a third-century governor of Lower Britain, Tiberius Claudius Paulinus, to a citizen of Gaul, Sennius Sollemnis, to whom he had promised an appointment. Sollemnis had defended Paulinus against accusations when Paulinus had been governor of one of the Gallic provinces, so Paulinus had hoped to provide a *quid pro quo*. In the event, no vacancy arose, so Paulinus sent Sollemnis the salary he would have received, together with some presents: 'You certainly deserve more, but I hope you will be willing to accept these few things from me, since they are offered to do you honour: a Canusine military cloak, a Laodicean tunic, a gold brooch with jewels, two coats, a British tunic, and a sealskin. Also I will send you your letter of appointment to the semestral tribunate, just as soon as a vacancy arises. The salary of this is 25,000

18

sesterces, which I want you to accept now, with the favour of the gods and of the emperor's sacred majesty. Later, you will receive something more worthy of your loyalty, in return for your services. Yours in friendship. . . .' The tribunate for which Sollemnis had hoped, which carried with it the command over the small detachment of legionary cavalry, did not materialise, and in the end he was summoned to Britain to serve in an unofficial capacity on the governor's staff. All Roman governors had some of their friends on their staff, to assist them with the administrative work. Such men sat on the bench with him at assizes. In addition, the governor had a large staff of lower-grade officials at his command. The lowest grade were educated slaves or ex-slaves, many of whom acted as stenographers or copyists, to deal with the mass of paper-work. Above these were a number of free men, acting as clerks and secretaries. A number of non-commissioned officers were normally attached to the governor's staff, seconded from military duties. Such were the *beneficiarii* and *speculatores*. The *beneficiarii*, in effect non-commissioned officers, commanded small police posts in strategic positions in the province, and could be entrusted with special commissions. The *speculatores* were couriers who were entitled to use the public posting service along the government roads which led from Rome to the provincial capitals to deliver official despatches, and, as well as their personal services to the

A speculator *on a tour of inspection*

governor, also fulfilled the function of public executioner. The governor had a full-time department of such regular soldiers, as well as civilians, some of whom would be slaves or ex-slaves. The soldiers often spent their entire period of service in very unmilitary tasks, such as the filing of records and despatches, writing letters and memoranda, keeping accounts—in general, office work.

Some 40 years or so after the establishment of the province a second administrative officer was appointed for Britain, the _iuridicus_. He was a man of lower status than the governor and under his overall authority, but his special task was the administration of justice in the civilian zone of the province. It is probably no coincidence that the first of these officials was appointed at about the time that the client prince Cogidubnus died. Probably the original need for the appointment arose from the rearrangement of the administration when Cogidubnus' realm was incorporated in the province. This came at a time when the governor was engaged in expanding the province's boundaries by war far to the north. The imposing residence recently discovered at New Fishbourne near Chichester, the capital of Cogidubnus, may well have been constructed as the official residence and headquarters of the new _iuridicus_, the first of whom was probably the eminent Roman lawyer and friend of the younger Pliny, Gaius Salvius Liberalis Nonius Bassus. The _iuridicus_ was retained as a permanent official, probably because it was recognised that the governor of a military province like Britain would never have enough time to devote himself sufficiently fully to civilian affairs. Nevertheless, it is clear that even in the military zone he must have delegated much of his authority to the commanders of the legions, and they in turn to the commanders of the auxiliary regiments, who in many cases must have had to act as district officers.

One sphere of the administration was kept quite separate— finance. The collection of taxes and all treasury business was in the hands of the emperor's agent, or _procurator_. It was quite common for governor and procurator to squabble, and the emperors found that the maintenance of two independent high officials gave them a useful check. Agricola, as a governor, always 'maintained a good working relationship with the procurators', according to Tacitus, but other governors, such as Suetonius Paulinus, disagreed with the procurator to their cost. The procurator Classicianus, a man of Celtic origin, evidently disapproved strongly of the repressive methods used by Paulinus after the suppression of Boudicca's rebellion, and was instrumental in securing his replacement by a governor of more generous spirit. From time to time certain procurators clearly had more sinister functions. For example, in 197, after the governor of

Tombstone of the procurator Classicianus

Britain, Clodius Albinus, had been defeated in his bid for the throne at the battle of Lyons, the Emperor Severus sent to Britain as procurator one of his wife's relatives, Sextus Varius Marcellus, who was an unusual choice. This man undoubtedly had as one of his main tasks the confiscation for the imperial treasury of the estates and property of the wealthy supporters of Albinus. In certain provinces at this time special 'procurators for the seizure of property' were appointed to deal with the estates of other political offenders. Such special appointments were not necessary in Britain, where the number of wealthy men was more limited. But from time to time other officials were appointed, for taking censuses prior to conscription, for collecting wild animals and gladiators for imperial circuses, and for other state business. Like the governor, the procurator had his own staff, some of whom were more or less permanently attached to the province, others that he brought with him. The procurator had to make arrangements for the collection of taxes, for paying the army of the province, and for supervising imperial property—estates and mines.

The seat of government from an early stage was clearly

21

London. In the first years Colchester (*Camulodunum*), the capital of the chief Belgic kingdom had been chosen, but within a short time London's superior geographic position told in its favour. It is here that the procurator Classicianus, who died in Britain, was buried, and the evidence of official inscriptions makes it plain that the procurators had their central office here. Other inscriptions record the presence of officials and clerks from the governor's staff in London. The natural result of this was that most of the main roads in the province radiated from this centre.

After the division of the province, York became the capital of *Britannia Inferior* (Lower Britain, i.e. further away from Rome). London remained the capital of *Britannia Superior*, Upper Britain. In the fourth century, the further division probably resulted in Cirencester becoming capital of *Britannia Prima*, London being capital of *Maxima Caesariensis* and perhaps Lincoln being the capital of *Flavia Caesariensis*. York was now capital of *Britannia Secunda*, and the fifth province, *Valentia*, was very probably a part detached from this—the zone round Hadrian's Wall, with its capital at Carlisle.

A large measure of local government was conducted by the Britons themselves with official supervision and encouragement. A number of towns were given the status of self-governing communities on the lines of towns in the Mediterranean world. Colchester, Lincoln and Gloucester were founded as Roman *coloniae*, chartered towns inhabited by Roman citizens—in their case demobilised legionary soldiers. The settlement which grew up outside the legionary fortress at York was eventually given this honorific status also. Roman St Albans (*Verulamium*) early acquired the status of *municipium*, inferior to that of *colonia* only in prestige. Probably London also at some stage acquired the status of *municipium* or *colonia*, although the details are not clear. These towns were administered by a senate (*ordo*) whose elected members (*decuriones*), nominally 100 in number, had to have a property qualification. The town senators elected annual magistrates from among their number, *duoviri* to preside over the senate and administer justice in minor civil cases, *aediles* to supervise public buildings, and to control local taxation and municipal funds, and probably *quaestores* also, to serve as secretaries of the Council. Every fourth year the *duoviri* were specially elected to conduct a census with the title of *duoviri quinquennales*. Another important official body was the board of *Augustales* who carried on the worship of the emperor, and elected their own officers, the *seviri*, annually. Each of these towns had a certain territory allotted to it from the surrounding countryside, which was taken from the territory of the British tribe within whose boundaries it lay. The new settlers of the *coloniae* were allotted lands in this area, and many were in effect owners of small estates which in some cases they farmed, in some cases let to tenants.

Other urban communities in the province had a different status. The Roman administration based their organisation on the tribal groupings that they found when they arrived, with one or two modifications and regroupings. The centre of each tribe (or *civitas*) eventually became a Roman town, but its inhabitants remained citizens of their tribe, not of the town. Thus the inhabitants of Wroxeter (*Vriconium Cornoviorum*) were not *cives Vriconienses*, but *cives Cornovii*, as were the inhabitants of other portions of the Cornovian territory. The town of Wroxeter, *Vriconium*, was simply the *chef-lieu* of the Cornovii. Similar rules applied elsewhere. Except that they lacked Roman citizenship—which Caracalla was eventually to grant to all provincials anyway—the *civitates* in most respects resembled *municipia*. The system worked well, and a few new *civitates* were created, even in the military zone of the Wall, where by the mid-third century the Carvetii of Westmorland had acquired their own *respublica*, with Roman-style magistrates.

A distinct disadvantage to the honour of being a town-

Inscription from Wroxeter, commemorating the new forum and basilica in 130

senator was that it was generally costly. The government expected the senates, composed of the wealthier members of the communities, to use some at least of their wealth for the public benefit. Specifically, the magistrates had to provide public spectacles, by virtue of their office, miniature versions of the grandiose shows in Rome. One result of this was to make service on the senate increasingly unpopular. At first it was probably sought after as an honour. By the end of the Roman period in Britain, men were even taking holy orders in the Christian church to avoid it, as may even have been the case with the father and grandfather of St Patrick. By chance, the only reference to Britain in the Theodosian Code is in a rescript of Constantine the Great, dated 20 November 319, which concerns the town senators, and, although the precise meaning is obscure, it clearly is connected with their financial obligations.

In most of the day-to-day running of affairs, the communities were left very much to their own devices. In certain matters they needed imperial authority. For example, permission to erect town walls had to be obtained from the governor and, from the reign of Marcus Aurelius, from the emperor himself. In some cases towns could obtain financial assistance for public buildings. Additionally, they were sometimes able to call on the skill and labour of the military architects and stonemasons of the legions. The town senates also had to maintain law and order with a small local police force. Only in certain areas was it necessary for the governor to place a *beneficiarius* with a small force, as for example at Dorchester-on-Thames, which was of course not a town with magistrates, but technically only a village.

The only corporate body for the whole province was the provincial council. The delegates to this were chosen from each of the *civitates* of Britain, and their duties and activities were largely ceremonial. They were, however, entitled to present a vote of thanks, or a vote of censure, to retiring governors. No details of any such votes have been recorded, although, as mentioned earlier, the governor Claudius Paulinus had been in danger of a vote of censure at the end of his term as governor of a Gallic province. The main function of the Council was a quasi-religious one, to attend ceremonies in honour of the emperor's divinity, held each year, at Colchester at first, for it was here that the Temple of the Divine Claudius was set up in the conqueror's lifetime (p. 138). At an annual festival, games, recitals, banquets and sacrifices were held, at the expense of the annually elected high priest of the emperor, as a profession of loyalty to the state. One other formal task which the council would carry out, was to invite some prominent Roman to become patron of the province. The names of one or two of these patrons are known, and they are those of men who had themselves,

An official sacrifice

or whose fathers probably had, served in Britain in some capacity in the emperor's service. In return for the honour of being invited to be patron, they were expected to keep a friendly eye on the interests of the province, and give legal advice and assistance if necessary.

By the time that service as a town councillor had become a burden instead of an honour, the pattern of life throughout the empire had changed enormously from the early days of Roman Britain. Taxation was very greatly increased, but the standard of administrators sent to Britain was lowered, and they were replaced with excessively regular speed. This meant that their opportunities for graft were increased. But the main offenders in this respect were the senior officials who now visited every province each year to collect the taxes on behalf of the central government. The town-senators had to undertake the unpopular

25

task of levying the taxes, and also of providing army recruits. The wealthier and more aristocratic members of the community were able to opt out of service as decurions by obtaining higher rank from the emperor, whereupon they could retire to their country estates. The unfortunate decurions, compelled to live in the towns, and to serve on the local senate in succession to their fathers—for it had become compulsory now for men in all walks of life to follow their family profession—were condemned to a life of unrewarding and unappreciated public service.

Meanwhile, the curious selection of governors sent to Britain in the fourth century were men who looked on the province simply as a place to endure while they could advance in rank, and the military commanders were in many cases Germans who were simply mercenaries. At the very end of the Roman period, Britain was, according to a Greek historian, 'an island fertile in tyrants', by which he meant usurpers. Some there were of these, such as Magnus Maximus, and Marcus, Gratian and Constantine III, who were hailed as emperor by the British army like others before them, and tried unsuccessfully to make themselves masters of the Roman world. But there were also springing up a number of minor princes on the fringes of the province. In the fifth century most of the province was under such men.

Further Reading

A. R. Birley, 'The Roman Governors of Britain', in *Epigraphische Studien* 4 (Bonn), 1967

E. Birley, *Roman Britain and the Roman Army*, 1953: Chapter Five, 'Roman Law and Roman Britain'

A. L. F. Rivet, *Town and Country in Roman Britain* (2nd. ed.) 1965: Chapter Three, 'The Roman Administration'

G. H. Stevenson, *Roman Provincial Administration*, 1939

III

The Army

The Roman army at its greatest strength was not much more than 500,000 officers and men, disposed for the most part round the frontiers of the empire. There were on average 30 legions, units whose normal full size was a little over 6,000, but whose fighting strength was about 5,000. Legionaries had to be Roman citizens, professional infantrymen serving 20-year engagements, which were in practice prolonged to 25 or 26 years; and in some cases men enlisted for further periods, especially if they obtained promotion. The auxiliary regiments of cavalry, mounted infantry and infantry, and a few specialised units of archers, slingers and the like, had a paper strength of 1,000 or 500 men, which was sometimes slightly exceeded. The officers in command were Roman citizens, but the men were recruited from among provincials without the citizenship, and sometimes among barbarians beyond the frontiers.

Approximately a tenth of the total armed forces of Rome served in the garrison of Britain, a surprisingly high figure, considering that the area of the province is very much less than a tenth of the total area of the empire, or even than the area of the frontier districts, and the land frontier in Britain was the shortest in the whole empire. Part of the reason lay in the undoubtedly unsettled and warlike character of the people of Britain, and also of their neighbours in Scotland, and across the Irish and North Seas. But Britain was also an important source of recruits for the army, and it may be that a province's garrison depended partly on the size of its contribution to the army.

Standard-bearers

After the arrival of the Sixth Legion, the legionary garrison took its final form: the Second *Augusta* Legion was stationed at Caerleon in Monmouthshire, guarding the Bristol Channel, and ready to move north into the Welsh mountains if need be; the Sixth *Victrix* ('Victorious') was at York, where it controlled the Pennines, and could be called on to reinforce the northern frontier; and the Twentieth *Valeria Victrix* was at Chester, from which it controlled North Wales and the western Pennines, and could keep a watch on the Irish Sea. Previously the legions had been stationed at other bases, such as Gloucester, Wroxeter in Shropshire, and Lincoln, and from time to time they were sent further afield, for example to Inchtuthil in Perthshire. But, after the building of Hadrian's Wall, they seem not to have altered their bases permanently until the very end of the fourth century, except for a brief period when Severus began the construction of an elaborate base of almost legionary size, at Carpow on the Tay. This was given up after his death at York in February 211, and soon after this Hadrian's Wall became the northern frontier once more.

Legions were divided into ten cohorts, and each cohort into six centuries, each commanded by a centurion, a professional officer, in battle the company commander, in peacetime responsible for training and discipline. Most centurions had risen from the ranks, although a few were given direct commissions. Below the centurions there were an enormous number of non-commissioned officers and soldiers with special duties and qualifications, with corresponding exemption from fatigues or higher pay. Some of these were attached to the personal staff of officers, others had subordinate positions within their century. The result was that it was not difficult for a recruit to rise with reasonable rapidity.

28

The centurions provided the backbone of the legions. With their swaggerstick, the vine-staff, with which they were entitled to inflict corporal punishment, and often with the gleaming decorations appropriate to their rank on their tunics, these company commanders were often much hated and feared by the men under their command. Many undoubtedly abused their position, and it was often the complaint of the legionaries that the centurions inflicted excessively savage punishment, and took money in return for granting leave or time off. But it was they who were chiefly responsible for maintaining the disciplined training which made the army what it was.

A centurion

The Romans connected the Latin word for army, *exercitus*, with the word for training, *exercitio*. All writers on the Roman army in ancient times emphasised above all else the Roman army's devotion to training. Foreign observers from nations defeated by Rome, like the Greek Polybius, and the Jew Josephus, and a Roman of the later Empire like Vegetius, anxious to revive the glories of the old Roman Army, in their different ways present the same picture. Recruits to the army were carefully selected for height, weight, physical strength and intelligence. Once recruited they were put through a programme of several months' rigorous training before they swore the oath that made them soldiers. The age at which recruits were conscripted or encouraged to volunteer was an early one. There is a case of a soldier of the Twentieth Legion who died at Chester, who joined up at the age of 14. But in general 18 to 22 was the commonest. The first thing the recruits were put through was the military marching pace. They had to be capable of marching 20 Roman miles in five hours of a summer's day at normal marching speed, and if necessary 24 miles at the faster pace. They had to learn to run at the double, to jump ditches and vault over fences. Above all, they had weapon training. They had to use weapons and armour which weighed double the normal amount, and with these practise against dummies set up in the parade ground. In particular, they were taught the use of the javelin (*pilum*) or throwing spear— 'against which no shield or breastplate were any use', according to Vegetius—and of the short sword (*gladius*). This was a stabbing sword, not a slashing sword: 'The Romans not only easily defeat those who fight with a slashing sword, they laugh at them as well.' The *gladius* only needed to penetrate two inches in the right place to be fatal. The recruits had their weapon drill twice a day, morning and afternoon, under the direction of the *campidoctor*. They had to practise putting the shot, swimming, vaulting the horse, the normal round of physical training.

Equally important with drill, route marches, weapon training and P.T., was training in engineering and pioneering work. Within each legion were men specially trained as sappers and pioneers, but every soldier had to be able to play his part in rapid erection of temporary camps and fortifications. They had to dig practice ditches for temporary camps. This was taken very seriously. The earth won from the ditch was to be piled into a rampart, into which wooden stakes were rammed. The work would be inspected, and measured by centurions, and careless work was punished.

From time to time, full-scale manoeuvres were held. The first-century army, at least, put its heart into them. Josephus commented that 'Roman manoeuvres are conducted as energetically as real battles without bloodshed; and to them real battles are simply manoeuvres at which blood is shed'.

Although the primary difference between the Roman army and the forces of their enemies consisted in the superior training and discipline of the Romans, there was also a basic difference in arms and armour. Very few of the peoples against whom the Romans fought had anything to match the protective body armour which both legionaries and auxiliaries wore, and the weapons of the Romans were equally superior. As well as his arms and armour, the Roman soldier on the march had to carry

Whitley Castle, near Alston: an exceptionally strongly defended fort

a good deal else with him—three days' rations, a saw, axe, entrenching tool, wicker basket for carrying earth and his own mess-tin. 'The Roman infantryman is as heavily laden as a mule', commented Josephus.

The same writer gives a detailed description of the army on campaign. Since the Roman commander-in-chief in the campaign which Josephus witnessed from the enemy side, Vespasian, had been a divisional commander in the invasion of Britain some 25 years earlier, it is probable that the reactions of Caratacus and his Britons would have resembled those of Josephus. 'The Romans never fight a battle until they have fortified their camp, which is erected in an orderly fashion. A great many craftsmen accompany the army, equipped with tools, and the ground is measured and levelled if necessary, the interior of the camp is divided into rows of tents, the exterior is made like a wall with towers at regular intervals, the artillery is placed between the towers, and there are four gates wide enough for baggage animals to pass through and for the army to sally out from. There are intersecting streets, the headquarters is in the centre like a small temple, there is a workshop quarter, tribunals from which the officers can address the men, and a ditch round the outside. Once dug in, the troops take their quarters in tents by their centuries. Fatigues are performed with the same discipline and regard for security. All take their meals at the same time at signals from buglers. At daybreak the rank and file report to

31

their centurions, the centurions report to the tribunes, and accompany them to the general's tent, where they are given the watchword and orders for the day. The signal to break camp is given by a bugle call, at which the soldiers strike tents and make ready. At a second call, they prepare to march and load the baggage animals. There is a third call to hurry the stragglers, then the herald asks them if they are ready. They reply three times: "We are ready!". Then the advance begins. The lightly armed auxiliaries and archers go in front to reconnoitre for ambushes and repel surprise attacks, then come a body of legionaries and cavalry, followed by the surveyors (*metatores*) with their measuring equipment, and pioneers to improve the roads and cut down obstructions. Then come the general and his staff with a mounted escort, followed by the legionary cavalry, mules carrying siege towers and similar equipment, other officers with an escort, and the legion's sacred emblem, the eagle. Then comes the solid main column, marching six abreast, with centurions keeping the ranks in step. At the end come the camp followers with the baggage train, the remainder

An army

of the auxiliary troops, and a rearguard of legionaries and auxiliaries.'

The artillery and siege equipment carried by the Roman army were on a small scale compared with the equipment of a modern army. But their catapults (*ballistae*) were more than a match for most of the enemies they came up against. Different types of catapult could direct a deadly shower of stone cannon-balls, arrows, or lead sling bullets against enemy fortifications. The Roman legion, as both Josephus and Vegetius expressed it, was an 'armoured city', which had to be completely self-sufficient, making its own roads and bridges, living off the land, but carrying supplies as well.

The words of Josephus can be illustrated very precisely by the scenes on the columns of Trajan and Marcus Aurelius in Rome, which depict the Roman army on campaign in graphic detail, on the march, with legionaries, auxiliaries, baggage train, and prisoners of war, foraging for grain, building camps out of turf, earth and timber, besieging enemy strongholds, and, of course, fighting. Traces of Roman military operations have

on the march

been found all over Britain, especially in the north and west. One of the native strongholds besieged by the force commanded by Vespasian was Maiden Castle: an excavation there has revealed the dramatic story of its capture. Another hill fort, Burnswark in Dumfriesshire, was besieged by two siege camps, one on either side. The gateways of the Roman camps were placed opposite the gateways of the native fortress with artillery platforms covering each one. In two or three places traces have been found of practice fortifications and siege works, such as those at Doldinnas in Wales, Cawthorn in Yorkshire and Woden Law in Roxburghshire—the latter a native stronghold which was no longer occupied when the Roman army set siege-works around it.

The commanding officer of each legion (*legatus legionis*) was a senator whose command over the legion was a part of his official career, normally coming at a stage when he was in his early thirties. His previous career would have included only one period of military experience, as tribune of a legion. The sena-torial tribune, technically second in command, was always a young man on the threshold of his career, generally not older than 21. He was normally appointed to a particular legion by

A British stronghold: Maiden Castle, Dorset

Building a turf and timber fort

the governor who was the overall commander-in-chief of the army of the province. In spite of the fact that these high officers could be described as amateur soldiers, yet, because the Roman state was always dominated by military ideals, because many of these senatorial officers dedicated themselves to their military duties conscientiously, and perhaps most important of all because the army was provided with a hard core of long-service professional officers, its efficiency was not impaired by the system of appointing the higher echelons of command.

There were two types of professional officers in the legion: the centurions, and the non-senatorial tribunes, of whom there were five to each legion, and who, although in some respects no more professional than the senatorial tribunes, had in many cases seen prior service as commanders of auxiliary infantry regiments. The auxiliary units were organised on a similar basis to the legions. The 500-man cohorts of infantry were the lowest grade. Above them came the 1,000-man infantry cohorts, then the 500-man cavalry regiments, and finally, the cream of the cavalry, the 1,000-man strong cavalry regiments of which there

A Roman cavalryman

was only one in Britain, the *ala Petriana*, stationed on Hadrian's Wall, at Stanwix near Carlisle.

The equestrian officers who commanded these units were ranked correspondingly. The commander of an infantry cohort of 500 men could go on to be an equestrian tribune in a legion, where his duties would be largely administrative—to keep the troops in camp, to bring them out for training, to keep the keys of the camp, to supervise the guard pickets, to supervise the standard of soldiers' food, to keep the quartermasters from cheating, to punish certain offences, to hear soldiers' complaints, and to visit sick quarters. If such an officer completed the full service open to him, he could end up as a commander of a cavalry unit, and very occasionally get the chance of commanding a double strength cavalry unit after that. Such men were the elite of the profession, and usually went on to high administrative posts.

Of the Roman army in Britain, the men who have left the clearest impression of themselves and their activity, and of their feelings towards the province in which they served, are the commanders of the auxiliary regiments, for the most part men of wealth and station, estate owners in their own provinces, doing several years' duty in the British army to gain themselves advancement. For a number of units a fairly full record has survived of the commanding officers' names, over certain periods: the prefects of the *ala Augusta* at Old Carlisle (*Olenacum*) in Cumberland for example. Another officer, who served near there at Maryport commanding a different unit, the First Cohort of Spaniards, dedicated an altar to the Genius of the Place, Fortune Who Brings Men Home, Eternal Rome, and Good Destiny. This man, Gaius Cornelius Peregrinus, came

Soldiers taking native prisoners

An officer's badge

from Mauretania, and while not wanting to offend the guardian spirit of the place, was clearly pining for home. But if commanding officers of his cohort were replaced as regularly as the prefects of the *ala Augusta*, he probably did not have to endure Cumberland for more than three years. Septimianus Rusticus, prefect of the *ala Augusta* in 185, had been succeeded in 188 by Tiberius Claudius Iustinus, and in 191 Publius Aelius Magnus, whose home was Mursa (Osijek in modern Yugoslavia), was in command.

Peregrinus could have had his family with him to make his life pleasanter, as did Rufinus, another prefect of the *ala Augusta*, whose son Latinianus joined him in dedicating an altar to Bellona the war goddess. Fabius Honoratus, tribune of the First Cohort of Vangiones, had his wife Aurelia Eclectiane with him, and their 'sweetest daughter', Fabia Honorata, was buried by them in Northumberland. The tribune Rufinus took his wife, Iulia Lucilla, with him to live in the fort of *Bremenium*, one of the outposts north of the frontier, in potentially hostile territory —perhaps the reason why a certain Eutychus, library clerk to the governor of the province, made a vow to the god Silvanus for their safety, or perhaps for their health. If so, the god did not protect them for long. Rufinus died at the age of 48 years, 6 months and 25 days, and was buried by his wife who took care to describe herself as the daughter of a senator. No doubt no other Roman senator's daughter ever lived so far north as she did.

Opportunities for advancement at most periods were open to the ambitious man who could find the right patron. Sometimes an influential senator could exert influence, sometimes the emperor himself could be approached. Tineius Longus, who commanded the cavalry garrison at Benwell, was 'decorated with the broad stripe (of the senator's toga) by the decision of our best and greatest emperors, under the governorship of the consular Ulpius Marcellus, and designated quaestor', thus entering on a senatorial career. Quite possibly he had the good fortune to be able to approach the Emperors Caracalla and Geta in person when they were in Britain in 211.

Caracalla, emperor 211–17

We do not know if the tribune Peregrinus continued his career as an army officer, but, if so, it may be suspected that he did not ask the governor of Britain for further advancement in the province. By contrast Marcus Maenius Agrippa, who had served his first period of duty as commander of a regiment of mounted infantry raised in Britain—the Second Flavian Cohort of Brittones—but serving overseas, was selected by the Emperor Hadrian himself to command the First Cohort of Spaniards, and his name is found on four altars dedicated at or near Maryport. His service in Britain won him promotion, and an obvious liking for the province, for he returned twice, first as admiral of the British fleet, and finally as procurator, and was able to record proudly that his son had entered the Roman senate. Agrippa may have taken satisfaction in the opportunity of doing some fighting; he was sent to Britain originally to take part in a campaign. This is certainly the impression given by Quintus Calpurnius Concessinius, prefect of cavalry, who 'paid his vow to a god whose spirit is very present, having slain a band of the Corionotatae', the latter an unknown tribe from the northern Pennines or from Scotland.

Commanders of some garrisons found hunting a pleasant relaxation from their duties. Marcus Aurelius Quirinus, prefect of the First Cohort of Lingones at Lanchester (*Longovicium*) in County Durham, as well as supervising the reconstruction of the collapsed headquarters building and armoury of the fort, and the baths and hall outside, completed in 242, spent some of his time up Weardale where he dedicated an altar to Silvanus the god of hunting. Quirinus was probably after wild boar, but he is unlikely to have had such success as a commandant at neighbouring Binchester, Gaius Tetius Veturius Micianus, prefect of the *ala Sebosiana*, who 'willingly fulfilled his vow to Silvanus the unconquered, for the capture of a boar of exceptionally fine appearance, which many of his predecessors had been unable to take'.

By the end of the first century, the army had begun to make itself permanent garrison forts and fortresses. Naturally, changes of policy, such as the building of Hadrian's Wall in the 120s, the new advance to the Forth–Clyde line at the end of the 130s, and the temporary reoccupation of northern Scotland under Severus at the beginning of the third century, made evacuation and new building necessary. From time to time, fire, whether accidental or caused by hostile attack, caused buildings to collapse. Sometimes, the records suggest, buildings long left unoccupied fell into ruin. In the meantime, the settlements outside the forts were growing at a fairly regular pace; and the urban communities of the lowland zone were always anxious to call on the masons of the army when they were available. There were, too, always the roads to maintain, as the milestones witness.

Thus the army was kept busy quarrying and building for much of its time. For the most part, the records of this activity are mute, or laconic. A legionary, quarrying stone for the Wall, carved on the crag face: 'The rock of Flavius Carantinus'. Two centurions and an *optio*, supervising quarrying half a mile north of Housesteads on the Wall, carved their names while taking shelter under an overhanging rock: 'The centurion

Distance slab from the Antonine Wall

Saturninus, the centurion Rufinus, Henoenus the *optio* (deputy centurion).' The Wall itself has provided many records set up by the building parties, recording the names of the centuries that did a particular stretch of the work, to satisfy the inspecting officers. More elaborate inscriptions were set up to commemorate building operations at their completion, honouring the emperor, and recording the governor, the unit commander and the regiment that had done the work. Thus at Netherby (*Castra Exploratorum*) 'the First Aelian Cohort of Spaniards, One Thousand Strong, Mounted, devoted to the emperor's divine spirit and majesty' recorded that the Emperor Severus Alexander had, in the year 222, 'under the supervision of Marius Valerianus the Emperor's Deputy, with Marcus Aurelius Salvius, Tribune of the Cohort, in command on the spot, built and brought to completion a riding school, the foundations of which had already long since been laid'. It is not recorded what the troopers at Netherby, outpost of the empire beyond the frontier of the Wall, thought of the language of such inscriptions. But in other provinces, where letters written on parchment or papyrus have survived, we can gain a more vivid picture of the feelings of individual soldiers. One man stationed in Arabia had been newly appointed to the post of legionary accountant, and wrote home: 'I give thanks to Serapis and Good Fortune that while other men are labouring all day long cutting stones, I, as an officer, stroll about doing nothing.'

Hadrian's Wall, with its attendant structures, was the most massive and impressive witness to the might, and engineering capabilities of the Roman army, even if in a sense, a confession of failure. For 73 miles from coast to coast ran a wall 15 feet high topped by a 6-foot battlement, 8–10 feet broad. On its north side was a deep ditch. At intervals of one mile were fortlets—milecastles—and between each pair of milecastles were two turrets. These, it is thought, housed a frontier militia, while the regular units of the army lay in forts at greater intervals, and devoted their time to training, while the milecastle men carried on the day to day work of customs and passport control. A metalled road linked these different elements, and the whole military zone was sealed off from the province by a great ditch

Hadrian's Wall, near Walltown Crags, looking east

on the south side bordered by earth mounds, the *vallum*. As time went on and even the frontier areas of the province became peaceful, the *vallum* was allowed to fall into disuse. For 40 miles down the Cumberland coast was extended a system of small fortlets and signal-towers. The senior officer, commanding the strongest auxiliary regiment, the 1,000-man *ala Petriana* at Stanwix near Carlisle, was at the west end of the Wall, and in its final form there were three outpost forts north of the west end of the Wall, as opposed to only two in the central zone and none at the east end. This indicates that the Roman High Command regarded south-west Scotland and the Irish Sea as the likeliest areas from which disturbers of 'the boundless majesty of Roman peace' would strike.

The legions in their permanent bases were housed in great fortresses, larger than many of the towns of Roman Britain, over 40 acres in extent, surrounded by a stone wall and ditch outside. Inside, the barracks, granaries, hospital, workshops, officers' quarters and administrative buildings were divided by a regular street system. The auxiliary forts were miniature replicas of the legionary fortresses. The most important building in both, the headquarters, was so placed that a soldier entering by the main gate would see ahead of him in the inner-most range of rooms the shrine of the standards with a statue of the emperor, the spiritual centre of his unit's life. The gateway of the headquarters led into a courtyard, on either side of which were the armouries. Beyond was a long hall with a raised platform at one end, from which the commanding officer would address the troops. Along the far side of the cross-hall were the rooms in which the commanding officer and his staff did the administrative work of the regiment, and in the centre, underneath the shrine of the standards, was the strongroom, where the unit's pay and savings were kept.

On one side of the headquarters building was the commanding officer's house, a comfortable establishment where his wife and family might live with him. On the other side were the unit's granaries, where the corn was kept in well ventilated barn-like structures. The barracks were not uncomfortable. They were in L-shaped blocks. In the end of the block lived the centurion in a flat to himself. The soldier in his *centuria* lived in a room which allowed more space per man than the British soldier was given until recently. The unit might also have its own hospital and workshops and, if it were an administrative centre for a region, warehouses where taxes in kind from the surrounding district

The fort at Housesteads, on Hadrian's Wall

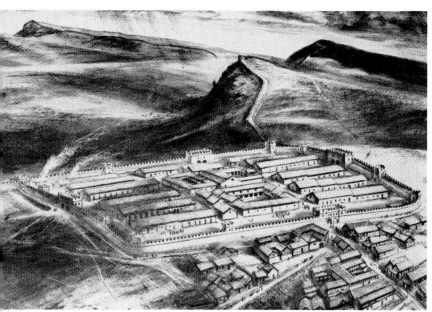

The military baths at Chesters, on the Wall

could be stored. Outside the fort was a very important feature of army as of all Roman life, the fort baths.

The legions which came over with Aulus Plautius in 43 were mostly recruited from Italy itself, with a sprinkling of men from the western provinces. The auxiliary regiments likewise were manned largely by men from the units' original homes. There was a motley selection, the Thracians from the Balkans being especially strongly represented in both cavalry and infantry units. Many cavalry units came from Gaul, particularly north-western Gaul, but there were other units from the Iberian peninsula, the Rhineland, Switzerland, North Africa, the Danube lands and Asia Minor. Soon, gaps in a unit's strength began to be replaced from the nearest safe source, then, finally, from among the Britons themselves. Thus, in the first century, Rufus Sita, the trooper of the Sixth Cohort of Thracians, buried at Gloucester, bears a Thracian name. But Sextus Valerius Genialis, a trooper of the First *ala* of Thracians buried at Cirencester not many years later, bore a Roman name, and was in fact a Frisian from the Low Countries, who had been given Roman citizenship, not a Thracian from the Balkans at all. By the second century, at least one Brigantian, a certain Necto-velius, son of Vindex, was serving in the army of Britain with the Second Cohort of Thracians in Scotland. The Brigantes were among the most warlike of the British tribes, and for that reason it is all the more significant to find him serving in the army very close to his home.

But at first the Britons recruited into the army were formed into new units which were sent to serve overseas, particularly along the Rhine and Danube frontiers. The warlike qualities of the Britons were recognised as being of great value to Rome, but it was thought wise at first, until the province had become more settled, to send them to serve far away from home. Even as late as the 140s, the re-conquered tribes of southern Scotland were deported en masse, with their families, formed into special army units (*numeri*) and made to live and serve along the frontier in Germany.

But by the second century, Britons began to enter not only the auxiliary regiments serving in Britain, like Nectovelius, but even the British legions. Julius Vitalis, from the *civitas* of the Belgae, whose capital was at Winchester, joined the Twentieth Legion at the age of 20, and died at the age of 29, having become a legionary craftsman. He was buried at Bath, which was presumably his home. A group of Britons serving in detachments of the Twentieth and Sixth Legions in Scotland, dedicated jointly an altar to the Mother Goddesses at Castlecary. Another British soldier known to us, Tadius Exuperatus, died at the age of 37 in an expedition against the Germans to which he had presumably been drafted. His tombstone, set up at Caerleon, also records the names of his mother and sister, and is revealing, because his mother, Tadia Vallaunius, bears the same *nomen* as her son, showing that he was technically illegitimate. His father was undoubtedly a soldier of the Second Legion at Caerleon, who had formed a liaison with a local woman.

Serving soldiers in the Roman army were not allowed to marry until the Emperor Severus altered the regulations at the beginning of the third century. But it was recognised by the government

Tombstone of Tadius Exuperatus from Caerleon

The emperor addresses his troops

that many soldiers, especially in peace-time, were bound to enter into common-law marriages with local women. To meet the legal difficulties which this would make at their discharge, the wives of those who had contracted such marriages were given Roman citizenship, if they did not already possess it, and subsequent offspring thus automatically became entitled to it. At first all their offspring had been given the citizenship on their discharge, but after a time this privilege was suspended, probably because the supply of recruits to the non-Roman auxiliary regiments had begun to dry up. Both before and after they were legally entitled to marry, soldiers of both the legions and the auxiliaries clearly experienced a happy domestic life. They had to live in barracks still—the army did not recognise marriages sufficiently to provide married quarters—but their wives could live in the settlements which grew up outside all the garrisons in the province. Some retired after their discharge to towns like London or Bath, where they no doubt set up in business. Others were content to live in the settlement outside their unit's fort, the *cannabae* or *vicus*. Such for example was old Julius Valens, a veteran of the Second Legion, who was buried at Caerleon, where the legion was based, by his widow Julia Secundina and son Julius Martinus, at the age of 100. In due course Martinus buried his mother who reached the age of 75. Julius Maximus, a junior N.C.O. of the *ala* of Sarmatians at Ribchester, was less fortunate. He buried his wife, Aelia Matrona, who died at the age of 28 years, 2 months and 8 days, his son Marcus aged 6 years, 3 months and 20 days, and his mother-in-law, Campania Dubitata, aged 50. Possibly all died from an epidemic.

Very few Britons seem to have attained high rank in the army. The highest ranking Briton recorded was a chief centurion of the Twenty-Second Legion at Mainz. Another British centurion, T. Flavius Virilis, served in all three British legions before being transferred to the Third *Augusta* and then the Third *Parthica*. While with the Third *Augusta*, he clearly took a liking to Numidia (Algeria) where it was stationed, and on his retirement settled there with his British wife, Lollia Bodicca, after 45 years' service. He died at the age of 70, leaving a widow and two sons. But in spite of the fact that no Britons are known to have reached higher rank, it would be unwise to conclude that none ever did. For example, it is quite possible that one of the Commanders of the Praetorian Guard of the second century, M. Macrinius Vindex, and his close relative, M. Macrinius Avitus Catonius Vindex, a distinguished senatorial general, came from Colchester.

In the second century, the government began to recruit new types of unit, like the Britons deported to Germany. Britain in turn began to receive irregular formations (*numeri*) of Germans and other wild peoples outside the frontiers of the empire. Frisians from the Low Countries, in particular, are found serving in several places, at Housesteads for example, where they were under the command of their own chieftain, Hnaudifridus (Notfried), and worshipped their own Germanic gods. At least some of these Germans brought their families with them. A certain Lurio had his sister living nearby to his unit. The historian Cassius Dio records that the Emperor Marcus Aurelius (reigned 161–80) compelled the Sarmatians from beyond the Danube, whom he had defeated, to provide 8,000 mercenary soldiers, of which 5,500 were sent to Britain. Some of these served at Ribchester in Lancashire.

The need to recruit men of this type arose from the increasing unwillingness of Roman provincials to enrol in the army. At the same time, the original sources of recruitment for the auxiliary regiments were becoming too civilised, and the sons of auxiliaries, if they wanted to serve in the army at all, would prefer the higher pay of the legions, in which, as Roman citizens, they were fully entitled to serve. After Caracalla's edict (in about 214) granting all free inhabitants of the empire full citizenship, anyone was entitled to join a legion rather than the *auxilia* if he satisfied physical and mental requirements. The government was forced to rely more and more on barbarians from beyond the frontier, so that by the mid fourth century even a number of high officers were of external, largely Germanic, origin. Such for example, was Fullofaudes, Duke of Britain, killed in battle against invading Picts, Scots and Saxons in 367,

Soldiers loading ships at a supply-base on the Danube

and such also was Stilicho, the commander-in-chief of all military forces in the West at the end of the fourth and beginning of the fifth centuries, and real master of the Western empire until he was murdered in a palace intrigue.

The regimental record office contained vast quantities of detailed records. Such irregular occurrences as the discharge of a soldier because of eye trouble were kept along with accounts of soldiers' pay, and details of how each soldier's time had been spent. One list of unit's strength gives a fascinating glimpse: one man had been 'transferred to the Dacian army'; another 'perished in the water'; a third man had been 'killed by bandits'. The pay records show how the soldiers had compulsory stoppages made against what they received—money was deducted for food, clothing, boots, Saturnalia feasts (i.e., more or less, Christmas dinner), burial clubs (paying for their tombstones on hire purchase with fellow club members to guarantee that they got a decent burial), and the rest could be banked with the standard-bearer to be kept safe in a strongroom underneath or adjacent to the chapel of the standards in the headquarters building. The soldier could draw out money to spend in shops in the camp village or local towns. But special bonus money issued by emperors (donatives) could not be drawn on in full. Half had to be banked.

The pay of the Roman soldier sounds meagre if the attempt is made to translate it into modern currency. But the attempt is in fact not worth making, for values have changed so greatly. The important thing was the enormous variations in pay according to rank and status. A legionary was paid three times as much as an auxiliary private. A chief centurion received more than 50 times the pay of an ordinary legionary. But the legionaries drawing basic pay only were probably not much more than half the strength of the legion. It was always fairly easy to gain gradual promotion, first simple exemption from fatigues with no increase in pay, then 50 per cent, and 100 per cent increase in pay with added responsibilities. From then on the soldier could specialise, becoming a clerk, accountant, signaller, medical orderly, armourer, any of a vast variety of functions. There were too positions

Medical orderlies at a dressing station

which required no technical skill, but good character and trustworthiness, such as being N.C.O. in charge of the watchword (*tesserarius*). The result was that many legionaries were already fairly wealthy when they retired. It was easy to save money when the legionary accountants automatically banked their pay and bonuses, and automatically docked their pay for food, and similar charges. When the legionary—and auxiliary—retired after 25 years, the emperor gave them a gratuity, often in the form of land and farming equipment with a small amount of capital. The government wanted them to become peasant farmers near their old garrison so that there would be a good prospect of sons following in their fathers' footsteps. Eventually, the government had to take steps to force sons of veterans to join the army as part of a whole scheme to tie sons to their father's professions.

The camp settlements where the soldiers could spend such money as they did not want to save grew up as soon as a fort was occupied for more than a season. At Housesteads the first settlement grew up outside the *vallum*, but before long this boundary was disregarded, and by the beginning of the third century the shops and inns were clustered around the fort walls. The shops sold a large variety of goods. At Housesteads there was a boot and shoe shop with a large stock of all shapes and sizes, for men, women and children. This clearly indicates that

A cutler's shop

long before the Emperor Severus (reigned 193–211) made it legal for soldiers to marry, they had set up unofficial establishments in the camp settlements. There was a seamy side to life in the *vicus* of Housesteads as well. A counterfeiter of coins was operating soon after 200, and about a century later a brutal double murder remained un-detected. A man and a woman were stabbed to death, and their bodies concealed beneath the

50

A souvenir from Hadrian's Wall: cup with battlement pattern and fort names

floor-boards of the back room of an inn less than 100 yards from the south gateway of the fort. The number of dice found suggests that a good deal of money must have changed hands at gambling sessions.

But as well as this kind of thing, there were shops which sold the necessities of life— food and clothing—and household equipment, such as crockery, cutlery and tools. Some shops on Hadrian's Wall seem to have made a special line in souvenirs. Two examples have been found of enamel cups, decorated with a battlement pattern, and bearing the names of some of the forts of the Wall. They must have been expensive items to buy, and probably were sold to officers. The normal camp settlement included a number of temples. The only religious building of any kind within the fort was the chapel of the standards at the centre of the headquarters block, so the soldiers had to satisfy their religious inclinations by clubbing together to establish small temples, or simply erecting solitary altars to the divinity of their choice. Many of the forts had worshippers of Mithras who were among the most highly organised of all. But most of the soldiers dedicated to their ancestral gods and goddesses. Alongside roads leading out of the settlement were the cemeteries. The towns outside larger forts, in particular naturally outside the legionary fortresses, grew to a considerable size. That at York, and perhaps that at Chester, were granted town charters. The town of Carlisle grew to 70 acres, not surprisingly as it was near the base of the *ala Petriana*, whose men, as troopers rather than infantrymen, from a double strength cavalry unit, represented the highest potential buying power in the entire area north of York. Another large town in the area was Roman Corbridge, which at 35 acres was larger than some of the smaller towns in the civilian area of the province. The reason was a special one. Corbridge housed a garrison of legionary craftsmen drawn from two legions. They operated in state factories which produced weapons, armour, tools and uniforms for the troops. With such potential spending power—

legionaries having much higher pay than auxiliaries—Corbridge also flourished with shops, temples, and inns. But it seems only to have been the larger places such as Caerleon, Chester, and presumably York, which were equipped with amphitheatres which could be used for military demonstrations as well as for mass entertainment. But there is little evidence for anything on a higher cultural level than such sporting manifestations as the amphitheatres would have offered.

Although the men obviously supplemented their diet from the shops in the civil settlements, their units provided food as well. They had to cook it themselves, and each of the ten mess rooms, which housed eight or ten men in the long barrack blocks, had its own hearth and oven where the men could make bread, porridge, meat stews, and anything else they fancied. It is a commonplace that the Roman soldier was a vegetarian. This may have applied to the Italian legionaries of Caesar's day, but legionaries from elsewhere, and most of the auxiliaries, clearly had a taste for meat. The profusion of animal and bird bones found indicates that they ate beef, mutton, pork and bacon, venison, chicken and game birds. Often oysters were eaten too, and no doubt fish, although traces of fish bones are hard to detect. For vegetables they would have less choice than nowadays, but some kind of salad such as fennel, varieties of lentils or bean, and cabbage were certainly eaten. They seem to have had cherries, apples, pears and probably many soft fruits as well.

The amphitheatre at Caerleon, Monmouthshire

To drink they could obtain plentiful supplies of home-brewed beer. But wine, no doubt much of it coarse and sour, was imported in bulk to satisfy the soldiers, and on occasion the quartermasters took special trouble over ordering. The Sixth Legion, when it was based at Carpow on the Tay at the beginning of the third century, must have had a lot of cases of chest trouble (not surprising in that latitude and climate), and special medicated wine, suitable for chest complaints, was provided.

When the army was not on campaign, and not training or engaged in building activities, it was increasingly diverted to various administrative tasks. Although most of Britain was

A wine-shop

divided into self-governing communities (*civitates*), there were a number of military zones which were obviously under direct military rule. Parts of Derbyshire, for example, were administered by the commanding officer at Brough on Noe, and in the highland zone of the Pennines in general most of the territory of the Brigantes, whose chief town and centre of administration was at Aldborough in the North Riding of Yorkshire (*Isurium Brigantum*), must have been under more or less military government. Such was certainly the case with the area round Ribchester in Lancashire, and the same clearly applied to the Hadrian's Wall zone. Parts of Wales were also under military rule.

In these military zones, the army had a serious policing problem. But even in the civilised part of the province, army detachments took over police duties from the often inefficient

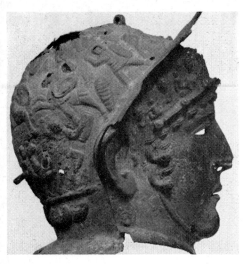

Face-mask helmet from Ribchester

local militias. Quite a large total of soldiers might be detached altogether for such miscellaneous duties. Some officers of the British army probably had the same kind of problem constantly facing them which an officer in Egypt tried to deal with: 'Domitius Julianus the centurion: On receipt of my first letter you should not have ignored it, but should have come to me, and informed me to whom the crops belonged about which the dispute arose. . . .'

The soldiers had no regular system of leave, although they could quite easily apply for leave with a fair prospect of being granted it. Nor was there any fixed, regular weekly holiday. However, throughout the year, at irregular intervals, but never much more than ten days apart, there were festivals connected originally with religious worship, particularly the primitive ceremonies of the old Roman republic, such as the worship of Jupiter the Best and Greatest, and Vesta, and other ceremonies dating far back into Roman history. In addition, there was an ever growing number of festivals honouring the reigning emperor and his family (his birthday, and anniversaries of his accession and so on), and others in honour of former emperors. Then there were ceremonies which affected the army itself more directly, such as the birthday of the unit, and ceremonies connected with the sacred standards, with the admission of new recruits and the honourable discharge of veterans. On many of these days there would be special parades. At the ceremony in honour of Jupiter, Best and Greatest, every January, the regiment paraded on the parade ground outside the fort, and their commanding officer dedicated a new altar to the god, while the old one was buried nearby. On such occasions the men had to turn out in their best parade uniform, which, for the cavalry especially, involved wearing elaborate face-mask helmets and white cloaks, and having their horses arrayed in extra finery. Although on such days there would be a relaxation of fatigues, the men probably enjoyed the extra work of cleaning uniforms and weapons, and practising drill and special formations, as much and as little as modern soldiers today. At least, they undoubtedly must have cut a dashing figure, with their feathered plumes in their helmets.

So far as is known, the army of Britain seems to have been reasonably contented for most of the time. There was one ugly incident in Agricola's campaigns in the 80s, when a unit recruited in Germany (in those days still exceptional) mutinied, murdered its officers, seized three naval vessels and fled, ending up after a fantastic voyage near the mouth of the Rhine. The next serious trouble came in the 180s. At the beginning of the decade, a governor was caught by surprise by the Caledonians and lost his life. He was replaced by an elderly martinet, Ulpius Marcellus, who instilled terror into his officers as well as into the men. In the meantime, the Praetorian Prefect in Rome was exercising an economy drive, and when they had avenged the death of the governor with a series of victories, for which they received no bounty, the soldiers grew mutinous. At the same time the senatorial officers commanding the legions had been replaced. The Sixth Legion was commanded by a hard-bitten ex-centurion who led a force of British legionaries over to Brittany to suppress a peasant revolt. The mutinous feelings of a detachment of British troops temporarily in Rome are said to have led to the overthrow of the unpopular Praetorian Prefect. But Pertinax, who replaced Marcellus as governor, nearly lost

Best parade uniform

his life in another disturbance, and when the governor of Britain, some ten years later, Clodius Albinus, made a bid for the throne, the British army for the first time fought against other Roman soldiers. It was not to be the last time. A more discreditable episode than this is the occasion in the fourth century when the frontier scouts of Hadrian's Wall gave treasonable collaboration to Rome's enemies, the Picts. But by that time, loyalties were breaking down all over the empire, and the government seemed no more than an oppressive and greedy taskmaster.

Further Reading

A. R. Birley, *Hadrian's Wall, an Illustrated Guide*, 1963

E. Birley, *Roman Britain and the Roman Army*, 1953

G. L. Cheesman, *The Auxilia of the Roman Imperial Army*, 1914

D. R. Dudley and G. Webster, *The Roman Conquest of Britain*, 1965

H. M. D. Parker, *The Roman Legions* (2nd ed.), 1958

P. Salway, *The Frontier People of Roman Britain*, 1965

G. Webster, *The Roman Army, an Illustrated Study*, 1956 (obtainable from the Grosvenor Museum, Chester)

Hadrian, Emperor 117–38

IV

Town Life

Among the many factors which distinguished the native Britons from their conquerors, the primary one was their lack of urban communities. Julius Caesar, in his two brief incursions into Britain, was able to notice that even in the limited area of the island which he saw, their nearest approach to a town (*oppidum*) was 'an area of woodland fortified by ramparts and ditches'. Some of these were on hill-tops, like Maiden Castle. Others, such as the fortified settlement which was probably the one Caesar captured, Wheathampstead, in Hertfordshire, covered an enormous area of flat land protected by forest and marshes. Into these strongholds the Britons could take their families and cattle in the case of enemy assault, to live for as long as an emergency lasted under the protection of a powerful chief, who might sometimes have his permanent headquarters there with his own family and retainers. The Gauls, Celts like the Britons, had similar strongholds. But by the time that Caesar conquered Gaul, permanent occupation had begun in many of them, and excavation has revealed some kind of town planning. This the Britons lacked, and even the new centres established between the invasions of Caesar and that of Claudius a century later, showed no notable advance. Cunobelinus' capital at Colchester (*Camulodunum*) was a vast collection of squalid huts and shacks. Even Cunobelinus himself probably lived in conditions which men of moderate means in the Mediterranean world would have regarded as squalid. Certainly he was wealthy, and was able to import expensive tableware, wines, and luxuries from across the Channel; had a mint producing regular currency; and exercised authority over a large proportion of southern England. But his capital was not what the Romans would have recognised as a town.

The whole civilisation of the Roman empire was based on urban life. Political thinkers and theorists in ancient times occasionally described the empire as a confederation of cities, of which Rome was merely the greatest. The Romans derived most of their philosophical thought from the Greeks, and the Greek philosopher Aristotle had described man as 'an animal that lives in cities'. At the time when Aristotle lived Rome herself was a collection of villages, inhabited by warlike peasant farmers on the fringes of Greek civilisation. In the centuries which followed, she overthrew and absorbed the mercantile empire of the Phoenician city of Carthage, the kingdoms of the east ruled by the successors of Alexander, and Greece itself. Enriched by conquest she gradually grew into the largest, richest, and most beautiful, or at least the most expensively adorned, city in the world. Rome herself was never planned scientifically by a town-planner, although the emperors did their best to give some shape and style to the ever increasing city. But where the Romans colonised, they built new towns on a regular pattern, copied probably from Greek ideas, but embodying their own genius for organisation.

The most characteristic Roman new towns had a chessboard

Silchester: 'a chessboard plan with a grid-iron of streets'

plan with a grid-iron of streets dividing the houses into blocks (*insulae*). At the centre was a market place (*forum*), with a hall for public meetings (*basilica*) and offices for the town council. Attention was paid to public drainage and water supply. Theatres and amphitheatres were often included, and public baths were an essential feature. The citizens of the empire were first of all citizens of their own town and were expected to play a part in its life.

In Gaul, Spain and Britain the Celtic peoples were not used to regarding a town as the centre of their lives, but in Gaul and Spain the influence of Carthaginians, Greeks and Romans had long been at work, so that the native communities (*civitates*) could be persuaded to form new urban communities. In Gaul the most obvious change was the abandonment of the hill-top strongholds in preference for sites on more level ground, more accessible to road and river trade and communication routes, and easier to build on. In Britain the Romans made a big effort to urbanise the country. It has been suggested that in the long run the attempt was unsuccessful, but during the centuries of Roman rule urban life did at periods flourish with great vigour for the first time in this country.

The first town which the Romans founded was at Colchester, Cunobelinus' old capital, the obvious choice as the new centre from which to administer a province consisting mainly of his former territories. For the first few years, occupation of the site was purely military, but in 49, six years after the invasion, the army was moved forward in connection with the campaigns in Wales, and a military colony was founded. The settlers were demobilised veteran soldiers from the legions which occupied the province. Their number is unknown, but was perhaps as many as 3,000. With their families, and slaves, and the addition of civilians from Britain and abroad ready to do business, the total population was probably very soon about 15,000. The character and origins of the hard core of settlers were undoubtedly Italian. The legionaries of this period—especially men demobilised in A.D. 49, who had probably mostly enlisted in 24—were predominantly Italian, particularly north Italian. Such for example was the centurion M. Favonius

Figurines from Colchester

Facilis who was buried at Colchester (p. 29), not long after the conquest by his freed slaves Verecundus and Novicius, and his stocky figure, broad face and sticking out ears are matched by a group of figurines from a child's grave at Colchester from this early period. The facial types of these people are matched again by the tombstones of a typical North Italian city such as Brescia.

Within the first dozen or more years a number of public buildings were erected at the new colony, including a theatre and council chamber (*curia*). But the town was dominated by a temple of the Emperor Claudius (p. 138), where worship was offered and games were held in honour of the province's conqueror. To the Britons, or some of them, this temple was regarded not as the symbol of Rome's civilising mission, but as 'the citadel of eternal domination'. The foundation of Colchester as a Roman *colonia* meant more than the building of the city. Large areas of agricultural land were expropriated from the surrounding peoples. The Trinovantes of Essex must have suffered particularly. It is uncertain how far the territory allotted to the colony extended, and as yet no certain traces have been found which are generally admitted to prove that this territory was centuriated—divided into strips of equal size on a regular system—after a complete survey. Indeed, it is possible that it was the absence of a planned confiscation that was an added cause of resentment to the dispossessed, as the new settlers may have had *carte blanche* to grab what they could. At any rate these were among the causes for the violent rebellion in 60 led by Boudicca, widow of the king of the Iceni. This is not the place to go into the details of the revolt, but its result was to leave Colchester, and the two other cities which had grown up, in ruins.

The sack of Colchester, St Albans (*Verulamium*) and London (*Londinium*) and the massacre of their inhabitants did not perhaps account for all the 70,000 lives said to have been lost on the Roman side, but it does suggest that the population of all three cities was at least 10,000. St Albans, which had been the chief town of the Catuvellauni until Cunobelinus transferred his court to Colchester, already had the status of *municipium* when was destroyed. This meant that it was a chartered town with its own council and magistrates and its own territory. At the same time the Catuvellauni continued to use it as their capital or chief city. London was an entirely new settlement, as the site had not been intensively occupied before the invasion. It was a largely spontaneous growth, peopled by immigrant traders, businessmen and money-lenders with their wives and families. The damage was restored, after the revolt had been suppressed, in all three of these towns.

A great many towns sprang up in succession to the trading settlements outside forts which, after a decade or so, were no longer necessary. Some, like St Albans and Colchester, had been settled previously. The first few decades of their existence as Roman towns did not see any great improvement on what had gone before. The population continued to live in wooden houses, and to use native pottery. It was in the 60s, after the suppression of Boudicca's rebellion had been followed by a period of milder administration, that marked improvements began. In the 70s and 80s building in stone was undertaken on a large scale, with active encouragement from the governor Agricola. In partial confirmation of Tacitus' account, an inscription has been found recording the completion of a public building at St Albans in the second year of his governorship.

In the last quarter of the first century, two further military colonies were established, at Lincoln for veterans of the Ninth Legion, which had been garrisoned there, and at Gloucester after the Second Legion had been transferred to Caerleon. These new foundations were about half the size of Colchester, and each was built on very similar plans. These were the last towns founded as an act of deliberate governmental policy in Britain. In the early third century the settlement outside the legionary

London, c. 200: already one of the largest cities north of the

fortress of York, which had grown into a town of some size, was granted the title of *colonia* to give it the dignity needed as capital of the new province of Lower Britain. Possibly Roman Chester, the garrison town of the Twentieth Legion's fortress, was given the title of *municipium* and there seems little doubt that London, which replaced Colchester as provincial capital very soon after the conquest, eventually acquired the title of *Colonia*—certainly before it was renamed *Augusta* in the fourth century. In that case it may well have acquired the status of *municipium* at an intermediate stage. Leicester, the centre of the Coritani (*Ratae Coritanorum*), may like St Albans have been the chief town of a *civitas* with the dignity of a self-governing town (*municipium*) as well, and the same may have happened to Silchester (*Calleva Atrebatum*).

The personal initiative of governors like Agricola un-doubtedly made a significant difference to the prosperity and

62

Alps, and the seat of government of the province

progress of the towns of Britain. But the biggest single impulse was given by the visit of the Emperor Hadrian in 122. The first reigning emperor to inspect the province since its conquest, he is said to have 'corrected many things there'. It is certainly obvious from archaeological evidence that in every town which has been investigated, a spate of new building followed his visit. No doubt after the legionary masons had completed work on the frontier wall, it was found possible to lend them, with military surveyors and architects, to the *civitates*.

St Albans was totally replanned, and its size was nearly doubled, making it some 200 acres in extent. At Wroxeter (*Vriconium Cornoviorum*) a grandiose new *forum* and *basilica* were begun, commemorated in 130 with an inscription set up by the council of the Cornovii in honour of the emperor (p. 23). Some state assistance was perhaps given for the work here. Not all the public building which went on in Britain was wholly successful. At Leicester, for example, there was certainly some inefficiency or lack of foresight, although the full details are not yet clear. As there was no spring close at hand for the baths, an ambitious aqueduct was planned to bring in water. But the surveyor got his figures wrong—the source of the water was 20 feet lower than the site of the baths. An attempt to remedy the discrepancy proved unsuccessful, and a water-collecting tower was built, fed from another source.

Nevertheless, in spite of difficulties such as these, the towns in the second century were flourishing, and imposing in appearance. Most of the chief towns of the *civitates*, as well as the colonies, London and St Albans, had their municipal buildings. These *fora* closely resembled the headquarters of forts in plan, another indication that they were built with military assistance. The citizens entered a courtyard, generally over thirty yards square, surrounded on three sides by colonnades, behind which were shops. The fourth side was filled by a long hall, the *basilica*. Behind this was a row of offices, in the centre of which, in the place where the chapel of the standards would be in the military *principia*, was the senate or council chamber, called after the senate house in Rome, the *curia*.

Apart from the shops and stalls in the *forum*, the most typical shop was a long narrow building, with a shop front at one end abutting on the street. The shopkeeper would also be a craftsman, and his shop would also be a workshop. If his clients found that the articles they required were not in stock, the shopkeeper could make them to order for the next time they came to town. The proprietors of such shops lived on the premises, generally, in all probability in an upper story, but sometimes in a few rooms at the back. The front end of the house would be his shop window, and he could open up his shutters to display

A cobbler at work

64

A draper's shop: customers looking at material

an open counter piled with his wares. There were rather more elegant shops in the *forum*, which had the advantage of the colonnade to protect their customers from the rain. As well as these shops there were naturally regular markets, to which country people could bring their wares, and to which travelling hucksters could bring their pack-horses, laden with imported pottery or fine bronze ware.

When the countryman came to town, he could find a useful selection of agricultural and household tools and the like on sale—spades, sickles, ploughshares, nails, hooks and shears. The metal caltrops found at Wroxeter belong to the military phase of the site—and are not a sign that Cornovian landowners had persistent trouble with poachers and trespassers. Townsman and countryman alike would find a plentiful selection of table crockery, cutlery and glass. Most of the finer pottery and glass was imported, but there was a regular supply of British-made wares, and in the second century mass production of high quality cups and bowls began at Castor, near Peterborough, which gained a wide sale in Britain and a certain success in Continental markets.

The houses of the upper classes were of far more elaborate

65

plan than the long, narrow, barn-like dwellings of the shop-keepers. Instead of the narrow-fronted gable-topped façade, they had two wings, making an L-shaped plan, with corridors along one or both sides of each to give more privacy to each room. The most developed style would have four wings, giving the house a private inner courtyard. Most of the larger houses were built on some variation of these plans. The most elaborate. such as the one at Wroxeter with private flush lavatories and private baths, had well over 20 rooms on the ground floor, whether or not they had an upper story. (For further details, see Chapter VI.)

Houses of this size and style were the property of the richer classes in the towns. These were of mixed origins, but our knowledge of them is largely impersonal, for it is the military areas which have produced the vast proportion of the inscriptions which cast a little light on the men and women of the time. There are more inscriptions known from Bath (*Aquae Sulis*) than from any Romano-British town, in proportion to its size. A small town of a little over 20 acres in extent, it was a health resort, whose hot mineral springs were well known beyond the boundaries of the province, and attracted a great many visitors. Many were soldiers on leave or convalescence from their units, or discharged veterans. Soldiers of all three of the main British legions are attested there, including several centurions, and a Spanish cavalryman who died there at the age of 46, less than a year after his discharge. Other visitors included a town councillor from the *colonia* of *Glevum*, and a man from the Moselle valley who was not a Roman citizen. Few natives of the town, in fact, are known, but Sulinus, son of Brucetius, seems to be one, for he takes his name from the goddess Sulis. He was a sculptor, and is recorded at Cirencester (*Corinium Dobunnorum*) as well. Another resident was C. Calpurnius Receptus, priest of Sulis, who died at the age of 75. But apart from people like these, whose work was connected with the spa or temple, the resident population of Bath must have been small.

The size of population of the towns is, indeed, a problem. If acreage is taken as the basis, comparison is possible, in the case of the *coloniae*, with foundations in other parts of the empire for which figures are available. On this basis, the new *colonia* at Colchester ought to have supported 3,000 veteran settlers, who, with families and non-citizens added in, would give a total population of some 15,000 for Roman Colchester; Roman London by the same reckoning would have 45,000 or more inhabitants. But not all the towns were equally densely populated. Silchester seems to have had a total of only 180 houses,

Mosaic from Leadenhall, London: Bacchus on a panther

although its area was as large as that of Colchester, the reason being that large areas were apparently unoccupied. For this reason, Silchester has been described as a Roman 'garden city', but this must be a misleading picture, for the unoccupied area will in fact have been filled with wooden shacks which would leave less easily recognisable remains than the shops and the substantial dwellings of the richer classes. In fact, the labourers and artisans who probably made up a large proportion of the town population have left little trace of themselves in comparison with the richer townsmen. They lived in wooden houses of very simple design, with home-made furniture, and little in the way of imported or shop bought household goods. But as townsmen, some of them acquired some degree of education. Tile factory workers, for example, had enough knowledge of Latin and of writing to scratch on wet tiles a sly dig at a fellow workman, such as: 'Austalis has been going away on his own every day for a fortnight.'

The richer classes in most of the Romano-British towns were undoubtedly mostly composed of men of British origin. Thus at Silchester one of the most prominent families was

Bankers

clearly that of the Tammonii. The first member of the family to
be given the Roman citizenship, no doubt as the regular reward
for his service as a magistrate, romanised his two Celtic names
into Saenius Tammonus, and no doubt had a *praenomen* as well,
to give the by now standard *tria nomina*. His son preferred to
make the family surname the principal name, no doubt having a
truer understanding of Roman nomenclature, and called himself
T. Tammonius Vitalis. A later member of the family, T. Tammonius Victor, shows by his names that this style was approved
by later generations. Tammonius Victor was married to Flavia
Victorina, whose names were completely Roman, indicating that
her family had received the citizenship from one of the Flavian
emperors. In some of the towns, notably the *coloniae*, the settlers
were of immigrant, military origin. At Lincoln (*Lindum*) Aurelius
Senecio the decurion and Volusia Faustina his wife bore completely Roman names, but they could well have had much more
British blood than descent from original Ninth Legion colonial
stock. There was another element in the citizen body as well,
immigrant traders. At Lincoln, Flavius Helius, 'Greek by
birth', and his wife Flavia Ingenua, were probably there through
commercial interests. This was, no doubt, the original reason
which brought M. Nonius Romanus from the Moselle valley to
Caerwent (*Venta Silurum*), perhaps representing exporters of
wine. Similarly, M. Aurelius Lunaris, a local dignitary of the
coloniae of York and Lincoln, who sailed from York to
Bordeaux in 237, probably did so for commercial reasons.
After Caracalla made all free inhabitants of the empire

68

Roman citizens in 214, their wealth alone distinguished such men from their fellows—although this soon became a legal distinction as well, between *honestiores* and *humiliores*. Those with sufficient wealth could go on to seek ennoblement in the emperor's service. Only one Briton is known to have achieved even the rank of *eques*, a certain Macrinius of Colchester, who could well be descended from colonial stock in any case, although his name is of the same type as Tammonius, suggesting Romanisation of a Celtic original. No senators at all of British origin are known, but the Macrinii Vindices who were prominent in second-century Rome may in fact have originated from the same family as the *eques* from Colchester.

Although drainage was an important feature of Roman town planning, only Lincoln is known for certain to have had a planned underground sewerage system, where every street had its own drain to which individual houses were linked. It may be presumed that the other *coloniae* were also provided for in this way, but the other towns had to deal with the problem in their own way. At Silchester, for example, there was no proper system, only street gutters and occasional wooden drains to carry away waste water. Similarly, garbage was disposed of in pits dug within the town. At St Albans, however, in the fourth century, garbage was systematically disposed of in the remains of the theatre, the use of which for this purpose is perhaps more indicative of a change in public tastes than of a decline in municipal standards—the theatre-temple had become a church.

If drainage was often primitive, attempts were made to provide a public water supply, even if sometimes, as at Leicester (*Ratae Coritanorum*), this was not very successful. Private houses often had their own wells, of course, for only those who could afford to pay for the privilege could have the public water main supply them direct,

Part of the sewers at Lincoln

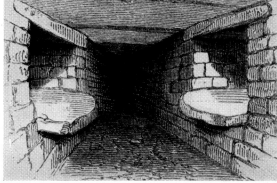

as was the case with the house at Wroxeter where the private lavatories were flushed by a sluice-gate which diverted water from the public main. But apart from providing drinking water, the most important function of the public water supply was to fill the public baths.

The public baths were an essential ingredient of town planning. If the Britons were to become Romans, and adopt the Roman, urban, way of life, they had to acquire a liking for a daily bath. The baths were erected at the expense of the *civitas*, and all were welcome to make use of them, although naturally those who lived in the town would have more opportunity to make a regular habit of it. The public baths were generally situated, as at Wroxeter, near the centre of the town, adjacent to the *forum* and *basilica*.

The bather entered the public baths through a courtyard of stylish design. In Britain, which had 'a foul climate' then as now, in the words of Tacitus, 'with frequent rain and mists', the porticoes were probably not often used to provide shade. From here the bather entered the changing room, where he could leave his clothes in a locker, and proceed to the baths

The large rectangular bath at Bath

proper. There were a great number of variations on the basic pattern of cold room, tepid room, hot room, sweating room and cold plunge. There was usually no provision made for swimming, except at spas like Bath. There were also rooms where the natural oils the body had lost through perspiration could be restored by a rub down with olive oil, which was then scraped off with a metal flesh-scraper (*strigil*). Here the pummelling by a masseur might go on as well. Ball games and other exercise might take place in the courtyard, or in a covered hall. The less active would settle for a game of dice and a drink. Officially, mixed bathing was frowned on, but the fact that

A bather's oil-can and strigils

edits had to be issued and re-issued forbidding it indicates that in some parts of the empire it was socially acceptable. But few public baths had separate establishments for men and women, and, when the edicts were being observed, men and women had to bathe at different times of day—very much as in the modern Turkish bath establishment, which in other respects still closely resembles the Roman system of which it is the direct descendant. But the Roman baths were very much more of a social club, where people expected to meet their friends and pass a few enjoyable hours.

Tragic mask from Caerleon

Apart from the baths, which acted as the main social club in the towns, there was from time to time public entertainment provided. Marcus Ulpius Januarius, aedile of the *vicus* of *Petuaria* (Brough-on-Humber), one of the small regional centres of the Parisi, provided a new stage for the theatre there at his own

71

The theatre at St Albans

expense in the mid-second century. Here the Parisi would have been able to attend performances of plays, mimes or pantomimes, dancing, singing and anything else which the magistrates could afford to bring to *Petuaria*. Remains of the theatre have not survived, but theatres at St Albans and Canterbury (*Durovernum*) have been investigated, and there at least they were planned on the conventional lines of theatres in other parts of the empire, with a semi-circular bank of raised seats for the spectators, a raised stage area in the centre, and a varying number of facilities for performers and audience. The wealthier citizens could rent their seats on a regular basis.

More popular than the theatres were the spectacular performances in the amphitheatre or chariot hippodrome. Judging by a lively mosaic of a chariot race in progress from a country house in Lincolnshire, the *colonia* at Lincoln, at least, was a venue for such events. This is confirmed by a fragmentary sculpture of a boy charioteer, found at Lincoln. Horse racing was not practised, but the chariot races round the long oblong track must have provided plenty of excitement. The boy charioteer from Lincoln probably performed in team matches between guilds of young men (*collegia iuvenum*), who

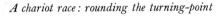

A chariot race: rounding the turning-point

were strictly amateurs. Few of
the British towns would be able
to keep up professional teams
such as excited the passions of
the population of Rome and
Constantinople, divided into
factions supporting the Blues or
the Greens. But some profes-
sionals clearly came to Britain
at times, judging by a cup found
at Colchester, on which is shown
a chariot race, with a caption
indicating that Cresces had won
('Hail Cresces!'), while his
three rivals, Hierax, Olympas

A boy charioteer from Lincoln

and Antilochus are bidden farewell. If their names are anything
to go by, Cresces was from the western, and his three defeated
rivals from the eastern, part of the empire.

Professional gladiators performed in the amphitheatres of the
towns, vast circular structures of which the largest was the
Colosseum at Rome itself. The provincial amphitheatres in
some of the richer provinces were on a large scale too, as
the remains at Nîmes and Arles demonstrate, but those in
Britain probably did not
seat more than 6,000
spectators at a time, and
the civic authorities
would be unable to
provide animals as exotic
as the lions and leopards
which delighted the
Roman plebs. Mostly
the enthusiasts would be
able to watch gladiators
fighting one another,
one traditional form of
combat being between
the man with the net and

Gladiators fighting

trident, and the fully armed man with shield and sword. One of these gladiators, Martialis, was buried at London by his wife. Martialis, or his wife, was from the eastern part of the empire like the three unsuccessful charioteers, judging from the Greek in which his tombstone was inscribed. A glass cup found at Colchester depicts four pairs of gladiators fighting, and gives their names. No doubt they were popular favourites for a time, and toured the western provinces. To vary the programme, there would be bear-baiting, bull-baiting, cock-fights and mock hunts.

It is not known whether the British cities and *civitates* were provided with doctors, as was the case with some towns in the empire. Certainly surgical implements were in use, but it is questionable how qualified the users were. One doctor is attested at Chester, dedicating, in Greek, the language of the greatest doctors of the times, to 'the gods who save'. His name was Hermogenes, and he may have been the emperor Hadrian's doctor, in which case his stay would only have been as long as the emperor's tour in 122. A number of patent medicines were on sale, all of them apparently oculists' ointments or lotions, such as 'M. Valerius Crescens' ointment for clear vision', and 'Q. Julius Senis' cream for soreness'; and there were a number which claimed to be suitable 'for any pain'. Eye trouble of various kinds is generally the result of diet deficiency, particularly in vitamins, and this was no doubt an underlying cause of the frequency of conjunctivitis (pink-eye) and similar complaints in Roman times.

Nothing is known of any regular state provision for education in Britain. Certain larger cities in the empire had state appointed professorial chairs and schools were sometimes set up with government encouragement. But there was no university in Britain—the nearest were in Gaul, at Bordeaux and Autun.

The only corporate religious obligation which a *civitas* had was to send delegates each year to the provincial council to participate in the ceremonies of emperor worship, and from time to time one of their delegates would be elected high priest of the province, which would involve him in a great deal of outlay, but would give him great prestige. The citizens were free to worship their own particular gods as, where and when they chose, but in most towns a temple quarter seems to have grown up, no doubt as a matter of convenience. As well as the native gods, such as the Saegon worshipped by the Tammonii of Silchester, the usual influx of foreign divinities found worshippers and temples. At London, there was a temple of Isis, the Egyptian goddess, no doubt founded by immigrant traders or sailors, which came to serve as a postal address, for a jug has been found inscribed *Londini ad fanum Isidis,* 'At London, by the Temple of Isis'. Few of these shrines had regular priests. Calpurnius Receptus,

'*At London, by the Temple of Isis*'

the priest of Sulis at Bath, was an exception, because the goddess of the healing springs on which the town existed naturally had a special place.

Most of the towns of Roman Britain, even some of the tiny communities which were smaller than modern villages, ended up equipped with massive walls. It is still far from certain when these walls were erected. The leading towns of the province suffered for their lack of defences at the time of Boudicca's great rebellion in 60, but even they were not given stone walls when rebuilt. One or two towns in an exposed position, such as Wroxeter and Aldborough (*Isurium Brigantum,* the chief town of those of the Brigantes who were administered as a *civitas* rather than by direct military government), may have been granted murage by the Emperor Severus or his son Caracalla. At this time the communities of the civilian part of the province had had to provide labour and money to help restore Hadrian's Wall, and after this task was completed men with sufficient experience would be available to carry out the task of town wall building in the south. But many towns seem not to have been given walls until later in the third century, perhaps by the separatist Gallic emperors, at a time when the attacks of the sea raiders were beginning. In the fourth century many of these

75

The city wall of Caerwent

walls were fitted with bastions to cope with sieges, and the communities that had been left unwalled were now brought up to the level of the rest.

In the first two centuries only earth ramparts and ditches had been thought necessary. Sometimes monumental gateways were erected over the entry of the main roads into a town, but these were for prestige, not defence, and the earthworks were probably of more use as a convenient city boundary than anything else. Later, runaway slaves and smallholders, as well as barbarian pirate invaders, made travelling without escort in lonely districts a dangerous business, and in the civilian zone the town constabularies maintained by the councils were incapable of dealing with the problem unless the towns were given the added protection of walls. The detachments of soldiers stationed at various points throughout the civilian zone were there exclusively for government purposes, for the most part to protect the public posting service, which was for official use only, and in certain cases to supervise the collection of taxes.

When the British towns were provided with walls, the area

enclosed within their circuit, although often smaller than the original extent of the town, was not such a startling reduction in size as was found in Gaul, where sometimes only a tiny perimeter round the public buildings was included. This and other evidence such as the signs of rebuilding in the later fourth century at St Albans, indicates that town life went on flourishing in Britain. Although the biggest developments came from the personal initiative of two emperors, Hadrian in the second century and Constantius I at the beginning of the fourth, the towns were capable of taking the initiative themselves, as the slight literary evidence for fifth century Britain demonstrates. Town life may not have reached the Mediterranean scale in Britain, but it was not a failure.

Further Reading

G. C. Boon, *Roman Silchester*, 1957

A. Fox, *Roman Exeter*, 1952

L. R. Merrifield, *The Roman City of London*, 1965

I. A. Richmond, *Roman Britain* (2nd ed.), 1963: Chapter Two, 'Towns and Urban Centres'

A. L. F. Rivet, *Town and Country in Roman Britain* (2nd ed.) 1965: Chapter Four, 'Romanisation—Towns', and Chapter Six, 'Political Geography'

Royal Commission on Historical Monuments (England), *Eburacum, Roman York*, 1962

J. S. Wacher (ed.), *The Civitas Capitals of Roman Britain*, 1966

V

The Countryside

The Romans did not bring with them any notable improvements in agricultural techniques. The heavier plough had already been introduced by the Belgae in the first century B.C. But in this, as in other spheres, the improved Roman organisation and centralised administration, combined with their superior building techniques, made a change in the external appearance of the countryside and an increase in the production of corn. The country dwellers formed the largest element of the population in Roman times, and throughout the Roman period a large proportion of the British peasants went on living in the same way as their pre-Roman ancestors, in the same simple timber-framed cottages or farmsteads, with very few changes to their way of life. If they were able to install the Roman heating system—*hypocaust*—it would be more likely to be used as a more efficient corn-drying plant than to make their living quarters more civilised. The Romans did of course build roads, for their own purposes, which made communications simpler, but this was of little value to self-supporting peasants who would need to use these roads mainly for bringing the corn demanded by the Roman government to the designated collection points. This corn levy was, at first particularly, often unfairly exacted, as Tacitus, describing the activity of the procurator Decianus Catus and his department, makes plain; and the discovery of an officially certified corn measure which in fact contains more than the quantity marked on the outside, seems to confirm the witness of Tacitus. The pattern of the countryside in Roman times largely followed that of earlier periods, dictated by the geology and geography of the countryside. In the lowland zone of Britain are found the Romanised farms which were mainly devoted to corn growing. In the highland zone of the north and west, the economy remained largely pastoral, and the raising of cattle, important to the Romans as a source of hides for leather, as well as for meat and milk, predominated, although clearly agriculture developed there under Roman rule.

A corn measure

The farmers of the Roman province were for the most part native Britons. But there were a number of exceptions. The *coloniae* had a large acreage of agricultural land assigned to them to be farmed by the veteran soldiers and their families. The expropriation of Trinovantian land for *Camulodunum* undoubtedly caused resentment, and the siting of the next foundations of *Lindum* and *Glevum*, while primarily dictated by the previous garrisoning there of legions, meant that the land taken from the tribes of the Coritani and Dobunni respectively, was of lower agricultural value, at any rate until the Romans took in hand a programme of drainage and tree-cutting. It is not known whether the Brigantes of the Pennines lost part of their territory to the *colonia* at York. At any rate, the citizens of Roman Colchester, Lincoln and Gloucester were men of Roman but not necessarily Italian origin who farmed their fields from their cities. This practice seems to have been followed by other Romano-British communities, for example, Canterbury (*Durovernum Cantiacorum*), for the countryside surrounding Canterbury has revealed few traces of farms, which indicates that the land was farmed from the town.

Certain areas of the province formed part of the imperial estates which were either farmed under direct governmental supervision by slave labour, or let out to tenant farmers under the overall supervision of an imperial procurator. Some of these estates had been acquired by the emperor in the early days of

79

Soldiers cutting corn for the army

the occupation, certain territories in East Anglia, for example, having been left to Nero in the will of the client king of the Iceni, Prasutagus. In the Fenland, the land was in any case almost unused until the Romans began drainage operations, which included the construction of a canal (the Car Dyke) to link the area by water transport with the Humber and Ouse, and thus with the legion at Lincoln—and later at York. Thus the troops could be supplied with corn from the imperial estates. It is just possible that an area in south-west England, round Salisbury Plain, was also designated as an imperial estate where corn could be grown to supply the needs of the Second Legion at Caerleon across the Bristol Channel. A similar arrangement may have existed in north-west England to supply the Twentieth Legion at Chester, although this seems less likely. In fact, corn grown on imperial estates was probably sold at its full market value abroad, and the British legions were probably supplied by native farmers through the payment of the corn tax (*annona*): imperial estates were run for profit, not to subsidise the British farmer. Other agricultural land was gradually acquired by the imperial Privy Purse as the result of confiscation of the property of politically undesirable landowners. A likely occasion for this to happen in Britain was at the end of the second century, when most of the wealthy men in Britain probably backed the wrong side in the struggle for power. Among estates which may have been confiscated at this time are one in Kent, where the family dwelling quarters went out of use, although farming of the property probably went on, and in Somerset, where an imperial procurator's agent records the rebuilding of the headquarters of an imperial estate in the years 212–17.

The best-known feature of country life in Roman Britain is the villa system. The term villa covers a very wide variety of farms and country houses built in stone in Roman times. Some were little better than farm cottages with out-buildings, others were enormous establishments capable of supporting at least 100 people. But all were devoted to agriculture, so far as can be told. They were not the pleasure villas described in loving detail by the Roman writer Pliny the Younger, country retreats for harassed townsmen. (In any case Pliny himself owned properties in several different parts of Italy, and some of these were intended to make money.) The occupiers of these Romanised farms were for the most part native Britons. One or two have been found on the sites of pre-Roman native farms of far more primitive design, and it is interesting to trace their gradual expansion and improvement with increasing prosperity and acceptance of the Roman way of life.

The majority of the inhabitants of Roman Britain were very little affected by Roman building techniques and superior material comforts. They went on living in farms not greatly differing from those that existed several hundred years before the Roman invasion. The best-known pre-Roman farm is one a little to the south-west of Salisbury, which is called Little Woodbury. The settlement enclosed an area of just over three acres protected by a wooden palisade against wild animals such as foxes. The farmhouse and buildings within this fenced-off area consisted of two circular structures, one about 50 feet, the other about 30 feet in diameter, constructed of massive

Winnowing

timber uprights, between which the walling was probably made of wattles or planks. As well as these two circular houses, or huts, there were a large number of pits dug into the chalk sub-soil, which were clearly grain storage silos. The harvested corn was dried on racks, and part was then set aside to be used as seed corn, and stored in granaries raised above ground level to ensure that the grain was kept dry and well ventilated, on posts, traces of which were found in the chalk subsoil. The grain which was to be used for consumption during the year was roasted in ovens, and then stored in the silos, some of which were as deep as six feet. The Greek writer Diodorus, commenting on Caesar's invasion of Britain, mentions that the Britons stored grain underground. The excavation of these pits has confirmed his evidence and removed the misconception that the ancient Britons lived in holes in the ground. Another salutary effect of the Little Woodbury excavation is the realisation that large numbers of pits can belong to a single farm. But it would be wrong to take this site as typical of the pre-Roman farm or of the 'native' farms which went on into the Roman period. The grain-storage capacity at Little Woodbury was large enough for at least three family groups; the people there possibly stored corn grown by farmers elsewhere—perhaps their tenants. In any case, nothing exactly resembling the Little Woodbury layout has been recognised from the Roman period.

In the extreme south-west, although the area was continuously under Roman rule from soon after A.D. 43, the effect on the agricultural economy was apparently almost non-existent. The native hut-settlements went on unchanged. In Dorset and Wiltshire some changes are marked with the Roman conquest—an increase in local roads serving rural communities, and the development of rectangular instead of circular houses. Some

settlements have recently been
detected in this region which
in plan resemble mediaeval
villages, laid out along a main
street, rather than the more
irregular prehistoric villages.
But associated with these settlements are fields of 'Celtic'
type (p. 6). It may be reasonable to state that taking the
country as a whole agricultural
prosperity increased during the
Roman period. But only the
better-off farmers can have

Ploughing

turned themselves into villa-owners. For example, the farmer at
Park Street in Hertfordshire kept slaves, as is indicated by a find
from the pre-Roman farm of a manacle with 37 links of figure-of-
eight shape. This future villa-owner, in the years immediately
preceding the Roman occupation, may have imported a certain
amount of pottery from the Continent, although it is difficult to
distinguish between the years immediately before and the years
immediately after the conquest; and some of the richer farmers
were obviously capable of buying wine. In the meantime, a
number of changes had been taking place with the growth of
larger settlements, such as that at *Camulodunum*. The Belgic
rulers dispensed with hill-forts except on their frontiers, but
outside their territories, in some areas, hill-forts began to serve
as centres of settlement for peasant farmers who could live
under the protection of a powerful chieftain.

After the Romans' arrival the hill-forts ceased to be occupied,
and they were in many cases replaced by towns founded in
plains. In some areas the land was clearly farmed from these
towns. But the pattern of rural settlement varied greatly. In
some parts of Britain where single farmsteads are rare, for example in the Fenland, villages certainly predominated. Where
single farms, whether Romanised or 'native' in type, are common, but villages have not been detected, the role of market-
centre and meeting-place was no doubt taken by the large

number of small towns which grew up at road-junctions, in some cases as posting stations to provide a change of horses for officials on tours of duty. Here traders became established who could supply the needs of farmers.

It was formerly thought possible to detect a continuous process of development in the type of farm buildings, and that there was a continuous progression from the Little Woodbury type of farm through varying degrees of Romanised structures to the fully developed villa. But it is a pity that very few of the 500 or 600 fully Romanised farms or villas can be shown to have been founded on the sites of native farmsteads of the pre-Roman period. Many sites all over the country, in fact the vast majority of farms, continued on the lines already laid down before the Roman conquest. The only changes made were improvements in water-supply, with the digging of deep wells, which made possible the keeping of larger herds of livestock through the winter. This in turn resulted in the construction of cattle-enclosures. Roman methods of corn-drying were also introduced, with, very often, the use of the hypocaust system. Nonetheless, it is striking how even in the primitive farms in Cranborne Chase (p. 96) Roman-style objects—bronze knives, brooches, rings and the like—began to be in regular use. At a very superficial level the Roman presence was all-pervasive.

Iwerne in Dorset shows a deeper, if still limited, influence of Roman ways. Here, a long oblong building, not quite rect-angular in plan, was constructed in timber, which showed an advance on the circular huts otherwise in favour. One end of this building, which was over 100 feet long, was partitioned off into three small rooms, the largest of which was only a little over 100 square feet in plan. These were clearly the living quarters, and the rest was used as a cattle byre. At the beginning of the fourth century this was replaced by a stone-built structure, slightly longer and a little narrower, but a truer rectangle. There were basically three rooms with a partially enclosed entrance at one end leading into a long room, 64 by 16 feet, which was clearly the byre. Two rooms led off this, the first with a flagged floor and the inner one with some painted plaster on the walls. Part way along the back wall a tower was constructed, which probably served as a granary.

The most luxurious villas seem not to have been constructed until the fourth century. But in the first century a number of small villas were constructed of strictly Roman type, or rather, of a type found in other western provinces of the empire. The basic feature of the design was that the farmhouse, essentially only a small three- or four-room cottage, had a corridor running along one or both long sides, which thus gave greater privacy to the occupants, as it was no longer necessary to pass from room to room to gain access. A good example of such a villa is that at Lockleys in Hertfordshire, where the original five-room house was improved by the addition of a corridor.

The corridor is so marked a feature of the standard Roman farmhouse in Britain that it has given its name to one type of villa, the 'corridor house'. A great many varieties of these houses have been found, some with one corridor only, some with one on each side. A natural further development for such houses

A country villa

was to extend one or both ends, thus forming wings, giving sometimes an H-shape, sometimes an L-shape, sometimes the shape of an E without its central bar. Very occasionally the fourth side was also built up, giving a completely enclosed courtyard. The farm buildings which went with these houses were generally of very simple barn-like design, and some farmsteads have been found where only this sort of building existed. However, even the basic barn design could be made more sophisticated, as is shown by an example from Hampshire, at Clanville. Here the dwelling house and two other detached buildings faced three sides of a roughly rectangular yard about 150 by 200 feet. The house was on the west side, a parallelogram of some 52 by 96 feet in size. Inside its design was remarkable, as the central space had been made into a courtyard, a columned space some 30 by 60 feet with an earth floor. On the long side was a narrow corridor cut in two by a cross wall, at the north end was a paved room and at the south end three rooms. Later, four rooms were added by partitioning off some of the courtyard. This type of building often occurs attached to corridor or courtyard villas, in which case it no doubt served as accommodation for the farm labourers. At Clanville, it is possible that the farmer was a small tenant on a large estate.

A good example of the medium-sized Roman British farming establishment is at Ditchley in Oxfordshire. Here, on the north side of a small valley running east to the Glyme, where the oolite and clay subsoil provides the basis for excellent corn-growing, was built a small six-room house on a very similar plan to that at Lockleys, but with the addition of two extra rooms at either end. Later, a corridor was added at the back, one end of which was partitioned off to make three small extra rooms, which probably served domestic purposes as kitchen, pantry and larder, for example. Curiously, no bath suite was discovered, but very probably one would have lain some distance from the main buildings, more favourably situated for regular running water. Later still, long stone verandahs were added, completely enclosing the house and giving it added elegance. The estimated height of the roof of the new verandah makes it clear that the rebuilt villa must have had a second

86

story. The house was set within a large rectangular enclosure, surrounded by a dyke.

The greatest period of prosperity for the farming community in Britain undoubtedly began in the fourth century, and it is from this period that most of the really luxurious villas come. One notable exception is the establishment recently discovered at New Fishbourne near Chichester in Sussex, where, after a timber construction of an earlier period (perhaps the granaries of a military installation of the invasion campaign) had been demolished, in about A.D. 75 well over two acres were provided with a solid platform of clay and stones, as a foundation for a stone-built house. Around a large, colonnaded courtyard, about 200 feet square, were constructed three, perhaps four ranges. On the north and east sides, each range had its own pair of courtyards, laid out as formal gardens. The west range was raised to a higher level, and the central room, probably approached by a flight of steps from the great court, and perhaps opposite the main entrance on the east side, contained a raised bench which has led to its identification as an audience chamber. The building was fitted, in a number of rooms, with mosaic floors of classical simplicity and elegance, and imported building stone was used, including marble from Carrara in Italy and from as far away as Skyros in the Aegean. No baths have yet been found of this early period. The reason for such unusual opulence and elegance of design in a first century house seems to be that it was an official residence, perhaps that allotted to the *legatus iuridicus*.

Even if few of the peasant farmers of Britain had enough capital to rebuild their farmsteads on Roman lines, it is probable that the majority of Roman British farmers were of British or

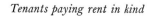

Tenants paying rent in kind

at least Celtic origin; if not native Britons, immigrants from the Gallic provinces. The new farmers who built the villas must have had capital. Some would be tribal notables given loans by the emperor Claudius or the philosopher Seneca, for example. Others would be businessmen who had made money out of the army of occupation with its enormous injection of new purchasing power into the economy. Such men as these would be glad to invest their profits in land, in the absence of any other outlet for it, except money-lending or trading ventures. There would be, also, after a time, veteran soldiers. The veteran colonists given land in the territories of the three *coloniae* founded in the first century have already been mentioned. There were, probably, however, one or two immigrant farmers from further afield. The way in which they came to Britain is not known, perhaps originally in the course of trade, or in some official capacity. At any rate, one villa which clearly seems to

Lullingstone villa in Kent: the modest

have been occupied by a family of non-British and non-Celtic origin is that at Lullingstone in Kent. The reason for this assumption is the discovery of two sculptured portrait busts done in a style commonly found in the eastern Mediterranean. There is a strong family resemblance between the two men depicted, and the style indicates that one was perhaps the father, or uncle, of the other. This would suggest that they formed, as it were, part of a collection of family portraits. The villa at Lullingstone was built on a low bank overlooking the river Darenth, with flint and mortar walls. The first house was of simple plan, probably constructed in the first century. At the end of the second century it was remodelled. A bath suite was added to the south end, and a new entrance to the north end. A room originally built as a cellar, on the river side of the house, was converted into some kind of loggia and the walls were decorated with painted plaster. Some of the rooms were

but stylish centre of a small estate

Portrait busts from Lullingstone

now given mosaic floors. The new owner who had these improvements made seems to have been the man who owned the family portrait busts. Although the house remained of modest size, with not more than half a dozen rooms, the bath suite, the mosaics, the wall painting and the portrait busts gave it certain pretensions. But its new-found elegance did not, apparently, last long, and it may be suggested that its owner, like, no doubt, many of the wealthier inhabitants of Britain, supported the governor Clodius Albinus with funds and encouragement in his unsuccessful bid for power, and reaped the consequences of his failure when the procurator Sextus Varius Marcellus arrived. No doubt this estate was confiscated, at the least, and the imperial privy purse probably let the land to a tenant content to remain in a far simpler residence elsewhere.

The house thus remained unoccupied for the best part of a hundred years, until about 280. It was shortly after this that the admiral of the British fleet, Carausius, set up an independent renegade regime in Britain, and one of his actions may have been to auction portions of the imperial estates as a means of raising ready cash. At any rate, at some time in the 280s, the baths were rebuilt, and the house reoccupied. The busts were placed with superstitious awe in the loggia, which was now sealed off. A generation and a half later, the house was replanned in a more elegant fashion. The corridor was split up, and its central portion extended to make a semi-circular recess leading into the central room of the house. This new main reception room was given an elegant mosaic floor, the theme of whose design was taken from classical mythology, depicting Bellerophon and the Rape of Europa, and above the latter scene an elegiac couplet referring to Virgil was inscribed (p. 163), showing that the new owners were men of some taste and education. The final developments are particularly interesting. In the middle of the fourth century one of the rooms was converted into a Christian chapel, decorated with wall paintings showing Christians at prayer in the traditional attitude, standing with arms outstretched. After some 30 years, the baths were filled in, but the chapel continued in use until the building was destroyed by fire at the end of the fourth century, or the beginning of the fifth.

The fourth century, the period when the villas were at their most flourishing, was probably the time when the vast establishment at Woodchester in Gloucestershire was founded, set on high ground on the eastern boundary of the vale of Gloucester, 12 miles from Cirencester (*Corinium Dobunnorum*), by then the second largest town in the province (or diocese, as the group of British provinces was by then collectively called), and a similar distance from Gloucester, the *colonia Nervia Glevum*. In its final form the Woodchester establishment was composed of two courtyard buildings joined together, with further outbuildings beyond, the area of the main buildings alone occupying as many acres as an auxiliary fort. The pride of the villa was undoubtedly the vast room in the centre of the northern range of the main block, the floor of which, over 48 feet square, was decorated with a square framed mosaic, within which was a circular design some 25 feet in diameter.

A favourite occupation of villa occupiers was undoubtedly hunting. British hunting dogs were highly prized in other parts of the empire, and the evidence suggests that they were much

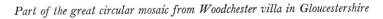

Part of the great circular mosaic from Woodchester villa in Gloucestershire

used in Britain too, for the hunting of wild boar, deer, and the wolf and fox. The dogs would generally be employed to drive the quarry into nets, so that they could be safely speared by the hunters. Lively representations of hunting scenes frequently adorned pottery and glass vessels of British and Continental manufacture, and a vigorous mosaic from a villa at East Coker

Hunting scene: mosaic from a villa at East Coker in Somerset

in Somerset depicts the huntsmen—or the beaters—returning with a deer slung from poles. One of the very small number of inscriptions from villa sites is, appropriately, a dedication to Silvanus, the god of hunting: 'C. Indutius Felix, willingly and deservedly fulfilled his vow to Silvanus, for the deities of the deified emperors, in the consulship of Victorinus and Gavius' (155). This dedication, like the mosaic from East Coker, also comes from Somerset, from Somerdale near Keynsham.

A good example of one of these villas which flourished to such an extent in the fourth century is provided by that at Llantwit Major in Glamorganshire. It is situated on the sea-plain of Glamorgan, four miles from the main road between the forts at Cardiff and Neath, some 250 feet above sea level, on ground slightly sloping from north-west to south-east. Its position was a little exposed, but there was a fine prospect in all directions, for it looked south to the Bristol Channel, less than a mile-and-a-half away, and on a clear day the coast of Somerset, 12 miles distant, is visible. The subsoil is Lower Lias limestone, between two and two-and-a-half feet below a mixed loam and clay topsoil. Just west of the villa, the ground falls away slightly, and the surrounding area is moist and liable to flooding, but the house itself was carefully placed just above the flood level. The surrounding land is now thought to be among the best for wheat-growing in Glamorganshire, and it is one of the most favoured positions in the country for climate, as the mean annual temperature of 51° is only bettered by the southern tip of Cornwall. The slope of the ground protected the house from the prevailing winds which vary from the north-west to the south-west.

The farmhouse and outbuildings at Llantwit were surrounded by a low bank and a ditch, probably more to protect the livestock against marauding wild animals than as any kind of defence against military attack. The villa was composed of four main ranges of buildings, grouped irregularly round a central yard, the whole complex covering an area of about one and a half acres. The buildings were of local limestone and sandstone, supplemented in places with imported Bath stone from across the Bristol Channel. The roofing material was mainly stone tiles, although some parts were roofed with red clay tiles. The windows had glass panes and the interior was decorated with fine plaster. The main rooms, at the east end of the north range, had floors paved with mosaics. There was a self-contained bath block, consisting of a suite of ten rooms, at the west end of the L-shaped main residential area. The remainder of the complex consisted of a barn-like building which was probably to house the farm labourers, as well as providing byre and stable accommodation, and a range of workshops. At some stage in the fourth century, the main residential block ceased to be occupied, and later, probably in the fifth century, a number of bodies were buried there. The labourers' quarters continued to be occupied, but the baths were adapted to use for the working of iron. This evidently indicates that the owners of the estate ceased to live there, but that the property continued to be farmed; in other words, it seems that it fell into the hands of an absentee landlord.

Llantwit is significant because of its position, adjacent to the military zone of Wales. In the fourth century a number of villas flourished in the military zone of the north as well, though none further north than that at Old Durham, just outside Durham City, so far as is known at present. The East Riding of Yorkshire, under the protection of the coastal defences system, was an area where villas notably flourished in this late period. It is almost axiomatic that there was a distinct economic difference between the highland and lowland zones of the country, but it is worth pointing out that more and more native farms which may almost be called Celtic villas are being discovered in the highland zone, which, although built on native plan, that is, circular rather than rectangular, were very probably devoted to corn growing and sheep and cattle raising for profit, in the same way as their counterparts in the south. It is often suggested that there was little corn growing in the north, but the meaning of the Celtic name for the fort of Birrens, an outpost north of the western end of Hadrian's Wall, *Blatobulgium* ('flour bag'), perhaps has some significance.

Grinding corn

The fourth century was certainly the heyday of the villas. It

94

A shepherd with his flock

is difficult to prove that any of the really substantial and elegantly equipped establishments were founded earlier than the end of the third century, although of course occupation of the sites had probably gone on uninterruptedly on a more modest scale from earliest times. In the fourth century British land-owners stepped up the export of grain, and the emperor Julian in the middle of that century had to take steps to improve the shipment of the normal loads of grain from Britain to the Rhineland. The villa at Hambleden in Buckinghamshire is one which very probably played a role in this production. Hambleden is a place where a sinister sidelight has been cast on social life in Roman Britain by the discovery of a large number of infant burials, indicating that there was a regular practice of infanticide over a prolonged period. But the evidence from Hambleden in the present connection is the large number of corn-drying ovens, indicating that corn was being grown on a very large scale. At the same time, a number of villas, particularly no doubt in the Cotswolds and in the south-west, had turned over to the production of wool. At Darenth in Kent and Titsey in Surrey, installations to process the wool have been detected, and fulling may have gone on at Hucclecote in Gloucestershire, in the centre of what was later the sheep country *par excellence*. (The traces of fulling thought to exist at Chedworth in Gloucestershire now appear to have been misinterpreted.)

Although it was emphasised at the outset that the Roman conquest did not introduce any fundamental changes into British agriculture, it is clear that the occupation did have a profound effect. In minor matters of technique, for example, the two-handled scythe and the iron-bladed spade seem to have been introduced by Rome, and their effect on the efficiency of harvesting and deforestation were undoubtedly marked. Rome did

95

not fundamentally alter the areas of cultivation—except perhaps in the Fenland—but the development of the heavier soils begun by the Belgic peoples was continued energetically. There were a number of manuals of agricultural practice by Roman writers, but these were naturally more concerned with conditions in the Mediterranean world. The most fundamental change which the Romans made was an economic one: there was under the Roman occupation for the first time an incentive to farmers to produce a marketable surplus—quite apart from the demands of the Roman grain-tax collector. It has, indeed, been suggested that this tax took from a half to three-fifths of the total yield of the poor peasant farmers in Cranborne Chase because of the reduction in the number of grain storage pits in the Roman period. But, apart from the difficulty of distinguishing the pre-Roman and Roman periods completely clearly in such cases, it is equally possible that there was a reduction of population, and, at the same time, a changeover from a subsistence economy to the cultivation of grain to sell at a profit.

Another change made by Rome was to the social structure. But it is still not certain what the relationship of the peasant farmer with his primitive hut to the villa-owner was. In some regions, the two appear to have been mutually exclusive, suggesting that there the peasants were tenants on imperial estates from which private landowners were excluded. Elsewhere both peasant and villa-owner are found side by side, in which case the former may have been the tenant of the latter. It is interesting to note that the sources do not speak directly of peasants' revolts in Britain on the lines of those which so troubled Gaul at different periods from the late second century onwards. But one writer appears to indicate that an outbreak in Gaul in the fifth century originated in similar trouble in Britain. This would not be surprising, in view of the subsequent close connections between Britain and Armorica, the future Brittany.

In spite of the large number which have been examined, the villas and their occupants are almost mute. A tiny proportion only of the inscriptions and *graffiti* from the Roman period come from the countryside, so that only a few names of the estate owners are known, or can be guessed, such as the Faustinus, whose villa in East Anglia was important enough to be recorded on an official roads' gazetteer, the Quintus Natalius Natalinus, whose name was recorded on a mosaic pavement at Thruxton in Hampshire, or the C. Indutius Felix, who dedicated an altar to Silvanus at Somerdale in Somerset. The owner of Chedworth villa may have been called Censorinus at one period, a name found on a

A peasant visits a businessman

silver spoon from there, but that is pure conjecture. The Lullingstone villa has at least preserved family portraits of its occupants. There is perhaps an indication of the identity of some of the ex-servicemen who became farmers, in the shape of their discharge certificates (*diplomata*), which are sometimes found in country areas. Reburrus, son of Severus, a Spaniard who was a troop-commander in the *ala Tampiana,* discharged honourably in 103, probably farmed a smallholding in or near Malpas in Cheshire, where his *diploma* was found, for these certificates were documents of great importance to the discharged soldiers, and would have been retained carefully by their families. It has been suggested that at Llantwit Major an absentee landlord may have taken over the estate at some stage in the fourth century. There is evidence from various sources of absentee owners of British land, apart from the extensive imperial estates, for example the noble lady Melania (St Melania the Younger), a correspondent of St Jerome. It is possible that one reason for the exceptional prosperity of Britain in the fourth century is that there was a flight of capital to the island from Gaul and the Rhineland. The Continental provinces were severely damaged by the barbarian invasions from the lands beyond the Rhine, in some areas permanently,

Travelling

whereas the various assaults on Britain had little more than temporary effect. In the fourth century the coastal defences only succumbed to one major attack (in 367), so that the island was perhaps a kind of haven of refuge: the contrast is made especially plain by the town walls of Gaul and Britain, for in Gaul the towns reduced their defended areas sometimes from 200 to 20 acres, a phenomenon which never occurred in Britain. The influx of Continental capital may have been the stimulus to the building of the luxury villas. At the same time, the export of corn from Britain to the Rhineland was a normal feature in the fourth century, which demonstrates the agricultural strength and importance of the country.

A still unsolved problem is the extent to which the villas survived the end of Roman rule, and to which the boundaries of their estates were perpetuated in Saxon land-tenure. One example, however, the villa at Withington in Gloucestershire is suggestive. Here, the study of other Roman sites and the natural features of the landscape suggests that the size of the Roman estate was about 4,400 acres, which is markedly similar to the estimated territory of the late seventh-century Saxon minster. This is perhaps not just coincidence. Several villas which have been carefully examined show a number of periods of occupation starting, in some cases, well on in the fourth century, and even though the later periods are difficult to date, as Roman coinage ceased to circulate, they may have gone on into the fifth, or even sixth century, which provides attractive evidence of continuity.

Further Reading

P. Corder, *The Roman Town and Villa at Great Casterton*, I, II and III, 1950, 1953 and 1961

H. P. R. Finberg, *Lucerna*, 1964

G. W. Meates, *Lullingstone Roman Villa*, 1955

I. A. Richmond, *Roman Britain* (2nd ed.), 1963: Chapter Three, 'The Countryside'

A. L. F. Rivet, *Town and Country in Roman Britain* (2nd ed.), 1965: Chapter Five, 'Romanisation—Countryside'

C. Thomas (ed.), *Rural Settlement in Roman Britain*, 1966 (Council for British Archaeology Research Report 7), *passim*

Mosaic from Bignor villa, Sussex

VI

Home Life

By the end of the first century the better-off Briton was probably
a town-dweller, who would have already become a Roman
citizen, or who would aspire to obtain the citizenship by being
first elected to the council and later serving as magistrate.
There was a property qualification for membership of the
council, and it was expensive as well as honorific to be a
magistrate. Such a man would live in a substantially built house,
either of L-shaped plan or built round a courtyard. Few such
houses seem to have had upper stories, but they had at least
ten rooms, connected by one or more corridors, to house the
family, which in Roman eyes consisted not only of wife and
children but also of household slaves. Even the middle classes
had two or three house slaves, who would perform domestic
duties such as cooking,
cleaning and stoking the
furnaces. Some at least
of the rooms were
heated by the standard
Roman central heating
system, the hypocaust.
In Italy itself this heating system was mostly
restricted to the heating
of baths, but in colder
climates it was widely
adopted for heating rooms

Hypocaust system of heating at Chedworth villa

'Venus' mosaic from Rudston, Yorkshire

as well. A stokehole on an outside wall fed a furnace with charcoal, from which heat radiated in channels underneath the floors, which were supported by stone or brick pillars, and up the walls of the room. Pliny had his 'den' in one of his country houses heated by 'a tiny little hypocaust, which by a narrow outlet retains or circulates the heat as required'.

A house with ten or a dozen rooms was large enough for the householder to keep separate rooms for separate purposes: he would build a dining room, a kitchen and bedrooms, and smaller rooms away from the main part of the house for use as slaves' quarters. The dining room in particular was often adorned with mosaic pavements on its floors, although the most elaborate designs were still rare in the first century. Later, with the spread of Romanisation, and, at the same time, clearly, a rise in the number of firms capable of installing mosaics, with pattern-books to choose from, they became more common. A favourite choice was a theme from classical mythology or literature. Normally there were five or six different colours of *tesserae* included in the design. A few mosaics illustrate the personal tastes of the occupant of the house, such as one from a country house on the Isle of Wight, which was clearly done to order for a man interested in mystical thought, particularly Gnosticism. In the fourth century, Christian, or quasi-Christian themes became popular. A newly discovered mosaic from Dorset shows the figure of Christ, beardless, with the Chi-Rho monogram in his halo. Orpheus playing his lyre, surrounded by wild beasts moving round in a peaceful fashion, was a favourite combination of a classical myth with a Christian theme ('the

101

Part of a decorated ceiling at St Albans

lion and the lamb lying down together'). The mosaic was set into a concrete floor, usually at least a foot thick, composed of a mixture of lime, sand and fragments of brick or tile.

The plastered walls were often painted in a variety of bright colours, with floral and architectural decoration. The furniture was often elaborate and elegant, if perhaps uncomfortable in some cases, by modern standards. The couch used at meals was generally made of wood, the legs being moulded by a lathe and about a foot high. There was a headrest and foot-board, and usually a back to it as well. Many were upholstered and covered with leather or cloth, and usually had cushions to support the left elbow. Couches do not seem to have been used as beds. Romans mostly slept on the floor, sometimes on a wooden chest or a raised stone platform. But they had mattresses at least, and blankets and pillows. But spring interiors were unknown. There is at least one relief, however, of what looks remarkably like a double sofa bed, with a married couple tucked up snugly in it under a capacious blanket or eiderdown.

Wooden benches with cushions were also used as seats, and women at any rate often sat on wicker chairs with rounded backs. There was also a type of high straight-backed chair with legs. Then there were stools of various kinds, including folding iron stools with leather seats. Tables were sometimes elaborately decorated with carved legs, notably, in Britain, of Kimmeridge

shale, an unusual
material. The furnish-
ing of the rooms was
completed by brightly
coloured table cloths
and candelabra. The
only form of artificial
light was provided by
candles or oil lamps.
During daylight hours
heated rooms were
lighted through glass
windows, which were

Terracotta oil lamps

not clear glass but translucent, serving the purpose of draught
excluders as well. Some families seem to have had *objets d'art*
of various kinds. Pictures have not survived, but there are a
number of what seem to be family portrait busts and other
pieces of sculpture. Each house had its own tiny shrine also,
with images of the household gods, the guardian spirits of the
family.

Before the fourth century, few of the villas reached more than
modest proportions, for it was only then that really wealthy
men began to live in the country and build the great houses of
which about seventy have so far been discovered in Britain,
and are often thought of as typical villas. Many of the earlier
villas had a dozen or so rooms, however, and the more prosperous farmers had their own bath suites, as it was impractic-
able for them to rely on visits to the town for regular baths. In
this respect they were better off than the town-dwellers, who
for the most part did not have piped water, and had to rely on
wells and water-buckets from public fountains for drinking,
washing and sanitation. Like the town houses the villas had
heated rooms and a certain elegance in their decoration and
furnishings.

The poorer classes in the towns, the craftsmen, shopkeepers
and the like, lived in more modest establishments, although
they too often possessed slaves. The standard type of house was
a long rectangular structure, with its narrow end on the street,

A small workshop

workshop at the back, and living quarters above. In the country, the poorer classes went on living in much the same way as before, uninfluenced in their daily life by Roman ways, except insofar as they bought mass-produced pottery, or exchanged their crops for it, and acquired a few trinkets.

If the newly Romanised Briton was to be a full participant in the 'higher civilisation' of Rome, he had to be well washed. Tacitus mentions 'baths' along with the other delights of Roman life to which the Britons became attracted under the benign rule of Julius Agricola, and the evidence of archaeology bears him out, although not all towns were equipped with large-scale public baths until 40 years or so after Agricola. Tacitus certainly meant public baths. Few town houses were equipped with private bathing suites, because the public baths were incomparably better equipped than a private house could be, and, besides, going to the baths was an accepted part of social life for all classes of society. We do not know how often the Romans took their baths, but it was certainly at least one a week. Seneca in one of his essays describes what it was like to live too close to a public bathing establishment (probably not something which that millionaire philosopher-statesman had in fact personally experienced, in spite of what he says): 'the sound of voices is enough to make one sick'. He lists all the various noises which disturbed him, the groans of men exercising with weights, the slap of the masseur's hand pummelling a man's shoulders, the splashes of noisy people jumping in, the sound of brawling, of a man calling out the score in a ball game, the cries of the sausage sellers and confectioners—adding, after all these items, 'it would disgust me to give details'. But of course those inside the baths were thoroughly enjoying themselves (see Chapter IV).

Thanks to the liberal policy of Agricola, according to Tacitus the Britons began 'to regard even our dress as honourable', and ' the toga became common ': the new Romans clearly took up—at first at least—the distinctive Italian formal dress for men, corresponding to our morning dress. The toga marked a man as a Roman, and the Romans sometimes called themselves *togati*, 'the toga-wearers'. It was in fact an expensive and not very comfortable form of dress, but it was still undoubtedly *de rigueur* for a Roman citizen in the first century A.D. for formal public occasions. It was made of fine white wool, in shape like two segments of a circle of equal size, placed with the straight ends together. Its length was nearly three times, and its width nearly twice, the height of the wearer, who had to fold it lengthwise and bunch it up into thick folds before putting it on, which was done by throwing it over the left shoulder with a third of the garment hanging in front. The remainder of the garment was passed across the back, brought round under the right arm and back over the left shoulder to cover most of the left arm. The back was then spread over the right shoulder and the front pulled up to form folds which made a useful pocket. Altogether a complicated procedure, but the Britons no doubt mastered it as easily as other peoples have mastered European dress. At least in the cold and damp province of Britain its warmth must have been less inconvenient than in Italy itself.

It was usual by the first century A.D. to wear one or more tunics beneath the toga (the

Roman dress

105

emperor Augustus, who always guarded his health jealously, wore as many as four). This garment was worn by both men and women. Women wore a brassiere underneath their tunic, which was longer than the men's version. Over this they could wear a *stola*, or longer tunic with sleeves and a broad flounce half covering the feet. Out-of-doors a square cloak could be worn. For normal outdoor wear men also wore a cloak of some kind, such as the *paenula*, a sleeveless square piece of cloth with a hole for the head and a hood attached. In the fourth century a special British hooded cloak, the *birrus Britannicus*, said to have been made of goat's wool, enjoyed a certain vogue in other parts of the empire, and must be presumed to have been commonly worn in the province of its origin. Hats were not often worn by either sex, as the folds of the cloak, or its hood, served to cover up the head in wet or cold weather. Up to the reign of Hadrian men went clean shaven, though probably not shaving every day, which was regarded as a somewhat effeminate practice. Hadrian, who wore a beard himself, popularised beards, which stayed in vogue for over a century. Women's hair fashions likewise followed the lead of the court, which did not however change very rapidly. The bun held the field for a long time, but at the beginning of the third century the oriental ladies

A lady being dressed by her slaves

ROMAN LEATHER SHOES

of the Severan dynasty popularised the wearing of the hair in ridges, either vertical or horizontal, sometimes as many as nine. Shoes were dispensed with inside the house. Out-of-doors men wore either heavy boots, with metal studs, for travelling, or sandals which laced up round the lower leg. A slightly

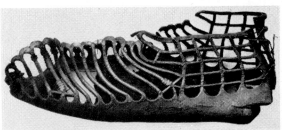

Footwear: hob-nailed boot and leather sandal

more elegant form was adopted by women. Within these types there was a good deal of variety, but high heels were not apparently favoured. The Celtic peoples were distinguished by love of bright colours in their dress, according to Roman writers, a characteristic which survives in the wearing of tartan, and even the Romanised Britons probably continued to dress themselves in slightly 'louder' clothes than the sober Romans of Rome.

Both men and women wore brooches, which were in the first instance a practical means of fastening. Mostly they were of bronze, in a great variety of shapes. Women wore bracelets, beads and rings as well. British pearls were supposed at one time to be valuable, but with the conquest the Romans found that they were of poor quality. Fans with ivory handles were used by some women. Jet ornaments from Yorkshire, in some cases pendants with portraits, were a particularly British form of personal adornment, although they were sold in Cologne also. The use of cosmetics was

Comb, carved with owner's name

A family meal

not widespread, but Roman women had their little bottles of perfume, tweezers for removing hairs, and other toilet articles.

The Romanised Britons evidently adopted Roman practice in taking their meals. Tacitus certainly tells us that they began to go in for 'elegant banquets' under his father-in-law's administration. Their day began early with a light breakfast, often taken before dawn. There being no infused drinks or beverages available, such as tea, coffee or cocoa, the normal breakfast was bread and fruit, with porridge in the winter no doubt. Very likely they drank some of the native beer as well (not a Roman practice). A light lunch was taken a little before midday, at which they might have eaten fish, eggs and vegetables, and drunk wine mixed with water. Again, the Britons certainly would drink their own beer on occasions as an alternative, a Celtic speciality which the fourth-century emperor Julian did not take to during his stay in Paris, in fact disliked enough even to compose a poem attacking it in satirical fashion:

ON WINE MADE FROM BARLEY

Who made you and from what?
By the true Bacchus I know you not.
He smells of nectar,
But you smell of goat.

The main meal of the day, dinner, began late in the afternoon, and was a leisurely occasion. A full-scale dinner was in three parts. First came the *hors d'œuvres* (*gustatio*, 'tasting'), of eggs, shell-fish (particularly oysters in Britain, where they were

108

plentiful) and salads, washed down with honey-flavoured wine. Then followed the main part of the meal, when there might be as many as seven courses, with the main dish coming in the middle. At one of the 'elegant banquets' of which Tacitus spoke, if not every day, the guests might have had roast boar, venison, veal and lampreys. Beef and mutton were not much eaten in Italy, but in Britain formed a regular part of the diet. No doubt, in a convenient fusion of Celtic and Roman customs, the practice of allotting the most favoured parts of the roast to

A butcher's shop: beef and mutton formed a regular part of the diet

the most honoured guests, common to both peoples, continued. Finally came the *mensae secundae* ('second tables'), with puddings, pastries, cakes, sweetmeats, fresh and dried fruit, and wine.

Most households made their own bread and ground their own corn as well, with a handmill. Wheat, barley, oats and rye were all used to make both leavened and unleavened bread. The resultant loaf was square and flat, much more like our wholemeal bread than anything else. Sometimes the loaves were spiced, or flavoured with honey or cheese. In the absence of sugar, honey was the universal sweetener. Salt, mustard and vinegar were normally on the table, but pepper was an expensive luxury. Numerous other seasonings, such as rosemary, thyme and garlic, took its place.

In the Mediterranean world olive oil was the staple cooking fat, but although it was imported extensively into Britain, butter and lard were also used. Fruit and vegetables were slightly less varied than today, tomatoes, oranges, bananas and potatoes being notable absentees. But otherwise there was a wide choice, apples and pears being the commonest choice. The quality of the fruit was probably inferior to that of today, for few farmers had the time or resources to devote themselves to experimental breeding and grafting, as did the former governor of Britain, Pompeius Falco, in retirement on his estates in Italy.

At the formal dinner at least, the Roman mode of eating was undoubtedly employed, reclining full length, supported by one elbow, on a couch or *chaise longue*, and eating with the other hand from a low table, rather than sitting up in a chair. The fork is a relatively modern invention, and in ancient times knives, spoons and fingers proved quite adequate for even the most elaborate dishes. For the first two centuries at least the favoured tableware was the coral-coloured glossy 'Samian', most of it imported from Gaul. There were as well native imitations of various kinds. Only the richer families could afford precious metal tableware; pewter was more

A dining couch

widely used. The great Mildenhall treasure, for example, must have belonged to one of the rich villa-owners of the fourth century. Glass dishes and drinking vessels also had to be imported, mostly from Cologne.

A drinking cup

Cooking was done on a charcoal fire in a raised stone hearth. Pots and pans were placed above small holes in the top. Portable ovens for baking were placed on top of the fire and more heat in a small brazier or the like was put on the lid. Mixing was done in bowls with a gritted interior surface (*mortaria*, 'mortars'). In the houses of the well-to-do the work of the kitchen was done by slaves, and it was the task of the lady of the house to supervise them and little more. She would not be expected to help her husband in his work—as a rich man he would be a property-owner or businessman—and could thus devote herself to the social round. Like her menfolk, she could go to the baths and to public entertainments, and received enough education to enable her to read and write, although few British women had husbands like Pliny who expected his young wife to comment on his literary compositions and set them to music on occasion. Most husbands

A silver platter, from the Mildenhall Treasure

A betrothal ring

would be content if their wives deserved the famous epitaph: 'she kept her home, she spun her wool'.

Roman marriage was strictly monogamous—as the soldiers' discharge certificates, with their reference to marriage 'one wife per man', piquantly illustrate, perhaps a necessary reminder to troops of non-citizen stock. (Divorce was, however, easy and very frequent among the aristocracy in Rome itself.) The age limit for marriage was 14 for males and 12 for girls. Young men usually waited a little longer, but it was very common for girls to be married in the 12–15 age-group. Before the marriage came a betrothal ceremony, with an exchange of gifts. This was not binding and could be broken off by either party—there was no 'breach of promise' action in Roman Law. It was the practice for the bride's father to provide her with a dowry, which, although it originally was held to belong to the husband, was later regarded as returnable to the wife in the case of divorce. The marriage ceremony itself began in the evening, when the bride was solemnly conducted from her father's to the bridegroom's house, escorted by a torchlight procession of relatives and friends, including married women (but restricted to those who had been married once only). Sometimes there was a double choir of youths and maidens who sung the marriage hymn '*Hymen, o Hymenaee, Hymen*'. The bride, who would have laid aside her girl's dress and dedicated her toys to the household gods shortly before, was dressed in a long white robe. Her veil was bright saffron, as were her hair net and shoes, and her hair was arranged in the style of the Vestal Virgins, to show three curls hanging down on each cheek. On reaching the bridegroom's house, she placed woollen fillets on the doorposts and anointed the door with oil. She was then carried over the threshold to cries of '*Talassio*' (a word of unknown meaning) from the throng of wedding guests. There were other ceremonies as well in the strictest form of marriage, but even the

112

The marriage ceremony

A family group

simplest usually had a marriage contract, signed and sealed by witnesses, and of course the guests were feasted.

With her marriage the Roman woman passed from the control of her father to that of her husband, but she was not in a completely subservient position. In fact, the Greeks, in their early contacts with Rome, noted with surprise the freedom of Roman women, for example that they participated in banquets with their husbands. Gradually, they acquired an improved legal position, until Christian influence encouraged women to take a more retired place. The emperor Augustus, who only had one child himself, in spite of three marriages, encouraged larger families, with privileges for parents of three or more children. But infant mortality was high, even in the upper classes—of Marcus Aurelius' children (he and his wife had at least twelve) only six reached adulthood. The discovery of infants' skeletons within town precincts may be an illustration of this, rather than evidence for the practice of infanticide, which did, however, exist. Insufficient hygiene was a contributory factor: an infant's feeding bottle made of terracotta, the nipple of which was covered with leather, must have been most insanitary.

Agricola took steps 'to educate the sons of leading men in the liberal arts', in his second winter as governor, and, although himself of Gallic origin, came to 'rate the untutored Britons higher than the Gauls. Those who had formerly refused to learn the language of the Romans, now began to desire eloquence in it.' Agricola seems to have brought a Greek schoolmaster, a certain Demetrius, from Tarsus over to Britain, and he went with the army at least as far north as York. He was probably not the only one of his kind, and there had certainly been instructors of Latin before him, however unwilling the Britons before Agricola's time had been, to polish up the rudimentary knowledge of the language which the inhabitants of the southern part of the island had acquired in several generations of contact with Rome before the conquest.

Home education

Presumably the young Britons were put through the conventional programme of education: 'as soon as a boy has learned to read and write without difficulty, it is the turn of languages and literature . . . the art of speaking correctly and the art of interpreting the poets . . . and every kind of literature must be studied. Omission of philosophy is a drawback', wrote Quintilian, tutor to the young cousins and heirs of the emperor of the day, Domitian. Both Greek and Latin literature were intensively studied—the Romans were avid students of Greek culture, although the Greeks were content to ignore Latin—and the aim was to produce a good orator, 'a good man skilled in speaking', as Cato defined it. It had a moral purpose, but in so far as it was practical at all, it was designed to produce a man fitted to take his place in public life, capable of speaking well in public. The principal method employed in the final stages was to set pupils the task of writing and delivering imaginary speeches, put into the mouths of historical characters, such as Alexander the Great or Hannibal. For the Britons, Latin remained an acquired language. St Patrick, kidnapped by pirates as a youth before he could finish his education, did not learn perfect Latin. Pelagius, by contrast, was familiar with a large number of prose and verse classics, secular and religious, and knew better Greek than

115

Arriving late for school

St Augustine. He is a tribute to Agricola, the founder of British education.

In the richest households there were educated slaves who acted as tutors to the children and taught them to read and write. Otherwise children had to go to a *litterator*, 'teacher of letters', getting up before cock-crow for the purpose. With him they used first of all a wax tablet and a stilus, so that their faltering first attempts could be easily and cheaply erased. Sometimes they scratched too deeply and left the impression of the letters on the wooden backing of the tablet. One person at least remembered a small portion of the school classics, in this case a bit of Virgil, for, scratched on a building tile, two words from the Aeneid—*conticuere omnes* ('they all fell silent')—have been recognised. Beatings were frequent and discipline rigid, although the court tutor Quintilian deprecated the practice. From the elementary school, the children—only the boys—went on to learn from the *grammaticus* at the age of twelve or thirteen. Here they learned to use pen, ink and paper, and studied history, grammar, literature and rhetoric.

Of the major events in life, birth, marriage and death, more is known about death in Roman Britain than the other two, because of the survival of tombstones and, indeed, of skeletons which often reveal the cause of death. To provide a tombstone was not, of course, cheap, but those whose private means did not ensure that they would receive an adequate burial very often joined a burial or funeral society, and paid regular, often monthly, contributions. These clubs had elaborate sets of rules: 'if any member has not paid his dues for six months, his claim to burial shall not be considered even if he has provided for it in his will.' Members met at regular intervals to have club-dinners, as well as business meetings, and had elected presidents, treasurers and other officers, as well as high ranking patrons. These clubs furnished a social need, and were one of the few forms of association permitted by the government, which suspected clubs or societies as breeding-grounds for seditious political activity.

Both cremation and interment were common, but whichever method was adopted the remains could not, under one of Rome's most ancient laws, be placed within town boundaries. Consequently the roads leading out of all towns became lined with tombstones, the Via Appia Antica of Rome itself being only the most notable surviving example. The tombstones followed a fairly conventional pattern. The inscription began with the formula *Dis Manibus*, soon abbreviated to *D.M.* ('to the gods of the shades'), followed by the name and age of the dead person, with, occasionally, details of his career, and, generally, the name of the person responsible for erecting the tombstone. Sometimes a few lines of verse were inscribed. But usually the inscription was simple, sometimes touching, such as the one for 'Simplicia Florentina, a most innocent being, who lived ten months. Her father Felicius Simplex set this up.' Those who could afford it had a relief carved with their portraits, sometimes with the tools of their trade, or partaking in a meal. The provident had their tombstones ready before death.

From the information on the

A family tombstone

117

A funeral procession (note the lifelike position of the deceased) : only the

tombstones, although they provide only a very small statistical sample, it is possible to suggest that the Roman Briton enjoyed a life expectancy roughly equivalent to that prevailing in twentieth-century British India—something in the 30s, low by modern European standards. Perhaps surprisingly, life expectancy was lower for women than for men, showing that women had a harder life in ancient times. Of course life expectancy varied a good deal from the upper to the lower classes. More of the better off must have lived to a ripe old age, even if they did not have such a pleasant existence as Pliny's friend Vestricius Spurinna, who, after a long career of public service, at the age of 77 was living a regular and ordered life of retirement, staying in bed for breakfast till after dawn, and spending the day in country walks and drives, and literary conversation with his friends. Some Britons may have

rich could provide for pomp and ceremony of this kind

approached, after a fashion, the way of life of Pliny and Spurinna—but only some. The Celtic peasantry—the majority of the population—had a humbler and harder life, which is little known from literary sources. Archaeology may eventually help us to know it better.

Further Reading

J. Carcopino, *Daily Life in Ancient Rome*, 1946
F. R. Cowell, *Everyday Life in Ancient Rome* (3rd ed.), 1964
J. Liversidge, *Furniture in Roman Britain*, 1955
C. H. B. and Marjorie Quennell, *Everyday Life in Roman and Anglo-Saxon Times* (6th ed.), 1961
L. M. Wilson, *The Clothing of the Ancient Romans*, 1938

VII

The Economy

The Roman emperors had nothing resembling an economic policy in the modern sense, unless they could be described as devotees of *laisser faire*. Their chief concern was to keep the various imperial treasuries as well filled as possible. The procurator of Britain, as paymaster of the British army, no doubt had little surplus from taxation to send back to Rome, but a number of specific taxes, such as the five per cent Inheritance Tax and the five per cent Manumission (setting free) of Slaves Tax were earmarked for specific purposes. The garrison of Britain and the general administrative machinery were paid for out of the levy on property. From time to time imperial edicts were issued to protect particular sections of the economy, but in general there were no state controls, even though there was not free trade in the strict sense, for the empire was divided into customs areas (*portoria*), and duty was also exacted on trade with the outside world.

The main difference made by Rome to Britain in this, as in other spheres, was the result of superior organisation. The building of roads, ports and lighthouses, and the intensive exploitation of inland waterways meant that trade could flourish as never before. The presence of the Roman army meant a large addition to the purchasing power in the island. A further notable difference was that Roman industry was organised on a capitalistic basis, producing for an indefinite mass market, while Roman banks and moneylenders were at once ready to give credit at what seems to us exorbitantly high rates

120

of interest to provincials anxious to improve their standard of living.

With the incorporation of Britain as a province of the empire, imperial coinage was at once adopted, and native mints ceased to strike, although the last native coinage did not go out of circulation until the second century. At the time of the conquest the Roman coinage which was to circulate in Britain was all struck in a central mint in Rome, administered by the emperor's treasurer. The currency was bi-metallic, based on the gold *aureus* of which there were 42 to a pound of gold, and the silver *denarius*, of which there were 84 to a pound of silver. One *aureus* was worth 25 denarii. The unit in which money values were reckoned officially was the brass *sestertius*, weighing one ounce, of which there were four to the *denarius*. The gold and silver coinage was divided into pieces of half value as well, and there were lower

The lighthouse at Dover

value brass and copper coins. Under Nero, Claudius' successor, began a diminution in weight of the gold and silver coin, and later emperors began the dangerous experiment of debasing the silver content of the *denarius*, until by the early third century it had only token value. Caracalla in 215 introduced a double denarius intended to compensate for this, but it too was of debased metal, and the process continued throughout the third century, producing dangerous inflation. After various measures by Aurelian, Diocletian reformed the currency in 296, and Constantine I introduced a new coin, the gold *solidus*, about 312. This restored confidence for a time, but it was symptomatic that it was not used as current coin, but had to be changed at a bank or on the black market. At the same time, the government wherever possible collected money taxes in gold or silver bullion at this period. In the meantime taxation

Coin of Diocletian

in kind became more and more prevalent. A notable example of the government's powerlessness and frustration in the face of inflation is Diocletian's Edict on Maximum Retail Prices, which attempted, in enormous detail, to restrict the prices of consumer goods, with apparently no effect whatever. Private individuals reacted to the economic crisis by hoarding the better value coinage.

With the increasing economic and military chaos of the third century, mints proliferated. The British 'Emperor' Carausius established several mints in the province, the chief being at London, and another probably at *Clausentum* (Bitterne, near Southampton), the main base of the fleet on which his independence depended. After the recovery of the province from his successor Allectus, an imperial mint continued to operate at London at various times. But the main mint which supplied the western provinces in this later period was that at Trier.

As well as being the ordinary medium of exchange, the coinage provided the emperors with the widest circulating means of propaganda then at their disposal. Their policies were advertised to the inhabitants of the empire in flattering terms, and at times of crisis the coin legends attempted to provide reassurance: *concordia exercituum*, 'the concord of the armies' was issued at times of civil war, for example, in direct contradiction of what was actually happening.

British metals had been expected to yield a large source of wealth to the Roman government, which exploited mines as a state monopoly. Tacitus calls them 'the price of victory'. The most famous British product of earlier centuries, tin, seems to have been little exploited by the Romans, for alternative sources of supply in north-west Spain had become available before the conquest, and the Cornish mines were not developed by them until the late third and fourth centuries. Only one Roman gold mine has been located, in Carmarthenshire, at Dolaucothi. In three main areas along the south-eastern slope

122

of the Cothi valley, veins of auriferous pyrites dipping at an angle of about twenty degrees were quarried by the most advanced techniques available. To clear away rock debris and wash the ore, an aqueduct channel seven miles long was engineered, capable of delivering between $2\frac{1}{2}$ and $3\frac{1}{2}$ million gallons of water every 24 hours. A supplementary use for this water was to provide pit-head baths for the miners. The Romans had clearly expected to find large supplies of gold in Britain, perhaps not realising that much of the gold that had reached them from there had been mined originally in Ireland and that area of Scotland which they were never finally to conquer. But at Dolaucothi at least they made the most of the gold that was in the province.

Julius Caesar reported that the Britons with whom he came in contact, those of south-east England, had to import their copper from abroad. But whether or not this was the case, the Romans exploited the copper resources of Anglesey and North Wales. A number of bun ingots of copper, of more or less standard shape and size, have been found there, some of them inscribed with Latin words, either names of concessionaires, or what in one case appears to be the title of a company. At Llanymynech in Shropshire, traces have been found of the dwellings of the miners. They lived in a cave attached to the mine itself, from which galleries with ventilation shafts connected them with the actual workings. This suggests that the mines were worked by slave or convict labour. But even convict mine-workers were normally well cared for, and the cave-dwellers were perhaps in fact refugees of the late Roman period.

The most widely exploited metal was lead. The Romans

Miners about to go down a shaft

123

A lead ingot

worked lead mines all over the country, not only for the lead itself, but for the silver which could be extracted from it. By 49, six years after the invasion, the mines in the Mendip hills were being worked, and these remained one of the chief sources. A mining settlement grew up at Charterhouse, where there was even an amphitheatre provided for the entertainment of the miners. Another extensive group of mines was on the borders of Wales and England in Shropshire, Cheshire and Flintshire. Derbyshire, the West Riding of Yorkshire and the moors round Alston in Cumberland were other areas where lead was extensively exploited. Many of the mines began and ended their existence under direct imperial control. Others were let out under strictly controlled terms, to private individuals such as P. Rubrius Abascantus and L. Aruconius Verecundus, both most likely immigrant businessmen, or even, perhaps, absentee capitalists controlling the mines from abroad. The mines of the Alston district were controlled very probably from the fort at Whitley Castle which was massively defended by a ring of nine ditches, probably extra protection required to protect silver bullion from raids by brigands in the Pennines. Lead remained one of Britain's constant exports. In the first century, the government official Pliny mentions in his encyclopaedic collection of miscellaneous information that lead was found in Britain in such quantities, including in surface deposits, that there was 'a law against it being exploited beyond a certain limit', possibly to protect Spanish mining interests. A number of ingots of lead with stamps indicating British origin have been found abroad, demonstrating that it was exported. The silver extracted from it presumably found its way to the imperial mint.

Traces of Roman iron workings have been found all over the country. At an early date the deposits in the Sussex Weald were exploited, and vast slag heaps have been found there. In places, slag from these workings was used to form the road surface in the neighbourhood, and the resulting metalling was not much inferior to modern tarmac. In the northern military zone the army worked locally on a small scale. At Stratford-upon-Avon there was an iron workers' settlement, and other traces or furnaces, slag heaps and iron blooms, have been found in the area. The only large concentration of the industry was in Herefordshire, notably at *Ariconium* (Weston-under-Penyard). Here, as in the Weald, wood, from the Forest of Dean, was naturally the fuel used to supply the smelting furnaces. But the Romans did not neglect the deposits of coal in this country. A third-century writer includes in his *Collection of Memorable Facts* the use of coal to make the sacred fire in the temple of Sulis Minerva at Bath. Shafts which must have been of Roman construction were noted at Benwell (*Condercum*) on the Wall sunk to a depth of 12–15 feet, into a two-foot seam which was then worked in every direction from the bottom of the shaft. At Housesteads one of the guard chambers of the east gateway of the fort was discovered on excavation to be full of coal (which the farmer there took away in a cartload and burnt on his fire). Excavation outside the fort has yielded traces of a coal bunker apparently attached to a cobbler's shop, so that the users of coal were many and varied.

An amphora

Wine had been imported into Britain in large quantities before the conquest. With the advent of the army and a host of immigrant traders accustomed to wine rather than the native British ale or mead, the trade was increased. The wine was imported in large *amphorae* or in barrels from Gaul and Germany. L. Solimarius Secundinus, from Trier, was one of the merchants who probably played a large part in the trade in the first century, and as he was buried at Bordeaux, he may have had a hand in the trade in claret and Graves, as well as his native Moselle wine. By the third century at any rate, British importers were handling the trade as well. One such was very probably

125

A wine-ship on the Moselle

M. Aurelius Lunaris, who dedicated an altar to a protecting deity at Bordeaux in thanksgiving for a safe voyage from York in 237. Lunaris was a *sevir* in the two *coloniae* of York and Lincoln. He could well have had a concession to supply wine to the Sixth Legion at York. M. Verecundius Diogenes, who originated from the Bourges district, was also a *sevir* at York, and may have handled imports of Burgundy. Attempts were made to cultivate the vine in Britain itself, although cultivation on a commercial basis was not permitted until 281 when the Emperor Probus revoked an edict designed to protect Italian viticulturists. Vine tenders' tools have been found in Britain and vine stocks have been found at a villa in Hertfordshire, but it is unlikely that the grapes were grown for the production of wine.

Drinking vessels of pottery, metal and glass were imported on a large scale. In fact, imports of table ware of all kinds formed a large item of the import trade into Britain throughout Roman times. In the period before the conquest the red glazed pottery from Arezzo in north-central Italy had already begun to find its way to the tables of the wealthier Britons. In the course of the first century its markets were taken over by manufacturers in southern Gaul, and crates of wares from their factories came over with the invasion army in 43. Sherds of Samian have been found at the base at Richborough. In fact, in the first

126

century they were being exported to
Italy itself, for unopened crates have
been found at Pompeii, which was destroyed in 79. The glossy red ware from
the Gaulish factories, known today as
Samian, continued to dominate the
British market for 150 years. Made in
a large variety of shapes, of which a
large proportion were decorated in relief
with floral patterns, or simple pictorial
scenes, these dishes, bowls, plates and
cups found their way all over the island.
A vessel carrying a consignment was
wrecked off the Kentish coast in the late

Samian ware

second century, and the profusion of pieces from the wreck
gave its name to Pudding Pan Rock. The vessels were often
stamped with the name of the potter, which gives some indication of the scale of their production. Men like Cinnamus must
have made hundreds of different moulds from which his em-
ployees turned out the finished products in kilns. The
dominance of these Gaulish factories suffered a severe blow
in 197, when many were destroyed by the victorious Severan
troops looting and pillaging after the defeat of Albinus, the
rebellious governor of Britain. In the third century, barbarian
invasion and civil war finally put a stop to the activities of the
surviving factories in Gaul and the Rhineland.

Production of pottery locally did not succumb to this competition. On the contrary, there was an increased market for
cooking vessels, mixing bowls (*mortaria*) and cheap crockery of
all kinds. In the second century production of finer quality cups
and dishes began in the Nene valley area. This pottery, known
once as Castor-ware, is now called 'colour-coated'. Its
decoration was applied freehand by the barbotine method rather
than made by the mould, and the scenes of hunting which were
the favourite theme of the Castor potters have a correspondingly
more* attractive and less mass-produced appearance. Attempts
were made to produce Samian pottery in Britain itself, notably
at Colchester, but it was the Castor-ware vessels which eventually

127

A Castor-ware pot

filled the vacuum left when Gaulish Samian declined in production. There were other centres where good-quality pottery began to be produced in the later period, notably the New Forest, and Crambeck in Yorkshire.

Castor ware found its way abroad also, notably to the Rhineland. A number of dealers in trade with Britain are recorded there, one of whom, M. Secundinius Silvanus, describes himself as 'a merchant in pottery trading with Britain' in a dedication set up near the mouth of the Rhine to a local goddess, Nehalennia, 'in return for the conservation of his cargo'. Another trader, a man from Britain named Fufidius, died at Kastel opposite Mainz on the Rhine. He is perhaps more likely than Secundinius Silvanus, who was a member of a rich business family from Trier, to have handled imports from Britain. The Secundinii were mainly concerned in the cloth trade, to judge from the representations on the elaborate family monument set up at Igel near Trier. Like other wealthy merchant families they invested their profits partly in land and partly in banking. There were no joint stock companies on modern lines, and banking activities, although they were sufficiently advanced to have credit transfer facilities, were in fact simple money-lending. The Digest of Roman Law indicates the variety of business which firms could transact, and one or two documents found in London demonstrate that commercial activity there was as developed as at Trier. Secundinius Silvanus most probably exported the glossy Rhenish pottery and glass which were sold in Britain in increasing quantities in the third and fourth centuries. The Rhenish jugs, vases and cups were made of fine thin fabric with a polished dark coating, and were often painted in white with convivial exhortations, such as 'long life' (*vivas*), and 'mix me a drink' (*misce mi*). The Rhenish glass ware is of exceptionally high artistic merit, either plain or coloured, or sometimes with an engraved decoration such as a particularly fine fourth-century example found in Somerset depicting a vigorous hunting scene with a pious motto of Christian inspiration running round the rim.

Bowl of Rhenish glass from Somerset

The army in this field, like most others, was at least partially self-supplying. A large legionary tile and pottery factory, run presumably by men of the Twentieth Legion, has been examined at Holt in Denbighshire, which includes, as well as workshops, barracks and a bath-house for the legionary craftsmen. Corbridge, the supply town of the Wall, has yielded traces of this as of many other industrial activities. Of particular interest among finds there are a potter's mould from which appliqué figures of a Celtic wheel god could be put on to pots (p. 137), and a piece of pot adorned with an appliqué figure from a similar mould, representing a smith god (p. 132).

Before the growth of Corbridge as a supply town, and even after it, local units continued to supply many of their own needs in this and other respects. A large concentration of pottery kilns has been found at Brampton in Cumberland of the Trajanic period, before the building of the Wall, which must have supplied the troops garrisoning the forts along the Stanegate between Corbridge and Carlisle. The tile and pottery kilns of

Glass tableware

129

A part-loaded Castor-ware kiln

the Ninth Legion near Carlisle must date from a similar period. In the third and fourth centuries pottery was produced at Housesteads and Chesterholm which seems to have been restricted to those forts and their *vici* in its distribution. Soon after the building of Housesteads fort a cobbler's shop was flourishing a short distance from its Wall, making shoes and boots of all shapes and sizes, and small workshops of this type and scale clearly flourished outside most of the forts as they did in the towns of the civilian area.

Fine silver tableware of the Roman period has been found all over Britain, most of which was probably imported from the Mediterranean or from Gaul, although the Capheaton *paterae*, for example, seem to be of British craftsmanship. Pewter table ware, which seems to have been particularly popular in the fourth century when silver was becoming increasingly costly, was certainly made in Britain, probably in London. Bronze vessels likewise were at first imported from the Mediterranean, later from Gaul, and finally were made in Britain as well, for example, at Lansdown near Bath where white lias stone moulds have been found.

Among other miscellaneous imports may be mentioned building stone, jewellery, millstones and earthenware lamps. The latter were generally fed with olive oil, which was also imported in large quantities for food and toilet purposes. Until the end of the second century Spain was the chief source of supply for the oil, which was exported, like wine, in *amphorae*, but after the defeat of Albinus the governor of Britain in 197, the estates of the olive growers, who had supported him, were confiscated, and their export trade seems to have ceased, or to have been diverted elsewhere. Thus the action of Albinus (which was responsible for the first disaster to Hadrian's Wall which was overthrown in the absence of the garrison) was also indirectly responsible for the destruction of many Samian factories, and the cessation of oil imports to the province he had governed.

Apart from Castor ware, British exports were largely of primary produce, raw materials which had been exported from Britain from earliest times. One industry which developed under Roman rule was the spinning and weaving of textiles. British textiles were sold on such a large scale even in the eastern provinces that they had to be mentioned in Diocletian's edict on Maximum Prices. In the fourth century there was an imperial textile factory at *Venta* (probably Winchester, rather than either of the other two British *Ventae*, Caerwent and Caistor by Norwich). Villas which had become cloth manufacturing estab-ments in the fourth century have been identified in Gloucester-shire, Kent and Surrey. But British specialities in this line had already become known by the early third century, when Claudius Paulinus sent a British *tossia* (plaid) among other presents to his friend Sennius Sollemnis.

Apart from a relatively small number of specialised imports, Britain was largely self-supporting. The ordinary requirements of life were supplied by the craftsmen and shopkeepers in the towns and countryside. Each farm had its own forge, and each town at least one blacksmith's smithy. At Malton in Yorkshire there was even a goldsmith at work whose shop was run by a

Transporting wine

Smith-god from Corbridge

slave. The only large wholesale industry which existed were the potteries, although some sections of this industry, such as that based in the New Forest, seem to have been run by independent craftsmen working on their own. Buying and selling was conducted mostly in the towns, in particular in their *fora*, but also in countryside markets. Only in the largest towns, like London, was there a developed commercial life. Here traces have been found of business documents: the brief sentence, 'this money shall by the terms of the claim be paid by Crescens or by the person concerned', throws a scrap of light on commercial life in early London.

Another glimpse of commercial activity in London comes from a letter from a certain Rufus, son of Callisunus, preserved on the wooden backing of a wax tablet: 'Greeting to Epillicus and all his fellow slaves. I think you know that I'm well. If you have made out a list, please send it. Keep a careful eye on everything, and turn that slave-girl into cash . . .' There is not much evidence for the degree to which slavery formed part of the life of the province. The evidence for their presence comes from the category of the more intelligent or wealthier slaves or ex-slaves. High up in the slave scale came Anencletus, who belonged to the Provincial Council of the province. He had married a free woman who had the Roman citizenship, Claudia Martina. Very probably she too had been a slave, and on receiving her freedom took her master's or mistress's *nomen*, the mark of her citizenship. Other members of this class who enjoyed a favoured position were Naevius, a freed slave of the emperor, who, as assistant to the procurators of Britain, was in charge of an imperial estate in Somerset, and Nikomedes, freed slave of the emperors, who made a dedication to Holy

132

Britannia at York, and was probably engaged in the administration of the province of Lower Britain.

The number of slaves in Roman Britain, and even their proportion to the rest of the population, remain hard to discover. But there were undoubtedly large numbers of them attached to the larger country estates, for example, and many of the artisans would use slave labour, like the goldsmith at Malton. Slave and convict labour was probably employed to a certain extent in the mining industry. One thing is fairly certain, that as time went on the supply of slaves from conquest dwindled, and at the end of the Roman period the traffic in slaves changed

Flask in the form of a slave boy

direction; Roman Britons, like the young St Patrick, were kidnapped by barbarians and taken to serve overseas. The existence of slavery undoubtedly played a part in reducing technological progress. It is noteworthy that the majority of water-mills, to take an example of a labour-saving device, seem to have been installed in the military zone where the army would have to rely on its own labour, even though individual soldiers might have had their personal slaves. The use of slave labour was not, of course, a Roman innovation, but Roman law did protect the status of the slave, so that his master did not have unlimited rights over his person.

It is possible to discover the identity of a number of the merchants and traders of Roman Britain. Some, such as Lunaris, Verecundius Diogenes and M. Nonius Romanus have already been mentioned. Rather more enterprising, and more exotic, was Salmanes, whose name indicates oriental, perhaps Jewish origin, who was living with his family on the Antonine Wall in Scotland, almost certainly engaged in trade. Another oriental trader in Britain was from Palmyra, the rich trading city on the edge of the Arabian desert. This man, named Barates, married a

Tombstone of Regina, a merchant's wife

girl from the Catuvellauni whom he had first acquired as a slave, no doubt in the market at *Verulamium*, and had freed and made his wife, giving her the name Regina ('queen'). Barates' trade was not, as might have been expected, dried fruit, but military ensigns, and appropriately he lived and died near Hadrian's Wall. Regina died at South Shields, the supply port of the Wall, where Barates had an ornate tombstone carved for her in the Palmyrene style. He himself died at the supply town of *Corstopitum* where his name and trade are recorded on a far humbler slab. One enterprising trader in that district whose name is only known in part (it ended -onianus) seems to have traded across the Solway or even across the Irish Sea, judging by a poem which he dedicated to a deity, promising that if success was vouchsafed to his venture, he would gild the lettering of his dedication. No traces of gilding survive, which perhaps indicates that it was a failure.

In general, it may be said that wholesale trade and industry was limited to a number of basic items such as food, drink, pottery and clothing, and most of the imports came from the nearest provinces, the Gallic ones. There were naturally fluctuations. Heavy initial loans by wealthy Romans soon after the conquest, military and political disturbances in the late second century with widespread repercussions, and an increase of capital investment in the fourth century, are three notable trends. In the late period, economic life became even more local than before the conquest: barter replaced money and wide areas returned to a subsistence economy, and those who could settled

134

down to survive the coming onslaught. But in this, as in every sphere of life in Roman Britain, more can, and will, be found out by the spade.

Further Reading

M. P. Charlesworth, *Trade Routes and Commerce of the Roman Empire*, 1926

O. Davies, *Roman Mines in Europe*, 1935

Tenney Frank (ed.), *Economic Survey of Ancient Rome*, Vol. III, 1937

H. Mattingly, *Roman Coins* (2nd ed.), 1960

I. A. Richmond, *Roman Britain* (2nd ed.), 1963: Chapter Four, 'Economics'

M. Rostovtzeff, *Social and Economic History of the Roman Empire* (2nd ed.), 1958

A steelyard weight

VIII

Religion

The Romans were catholic in the widest sense in their attitude
to religion. Each man and each people could worship their own
gods, a rule to which very few exceptions were made in the
case of practices to which the government objected on political
or humanitarian grounds. As a result, the Britons went on
worshipping their ancestral Celtic deities throughout the
Roman period, and the immigrants of different classes and
national origins brought with them a motley host of new creeds,
some of which attracted British worshippers. The Britons, like
other Celts, worshipped the spirits of nature. Sea and sky,
mountains, rivers and trees were thought to be endowed with
powerful spirits who could be placated and persuaded to influence events in favour of the worshipper by prayer and
sacrifice. The pig, bull, horse and serpent were also regarded as
possessing supernatural powers, and the sun, the source of heat
and light, and the moon, the measure of time, were closely
studied.

In these respects, Celtic religion was not unlike that of other
pagan peoples, and the Romans, with their ready tolerance, did
not find it difficult to identify the gods and spirits of Celtic
Britain with members of their own Pantheon. But the Celts also
had an organised priesthood, which was exceptional—the
Druids. The Celts worshipped in sacred groves, which sometimes included an image of the god, and even a simple wooden
temple. Sometimes also, human sacrifice might take place there,
and the Druids would make prophecies after interpreting the

twitching of the victim's limbs and the flow of his blood. It was this practice of human sacrifice, as well as the political influence exercised by the Druids in their capacity as tribal judges, that led the Romans to prohibit their activity, and ruthlessly to exterminate resisters. Britain as a whole was looked to by other Celtic peoples as a special home of the Druidical lore, and in Britain the sacred island of Anglesey (*Mona*) was their particular stronghold. The governor Suetonius Paulinus was in fact engaged in an assault on *Mona*, and in destroying the sacred groves of the Druids, when Boudicca rebelled in 60. It is not unlikely that the Roman assault on the citadel of her ancestral religion was an added incentive, as well as a convenient

The Celtic wheel god Taranis

opportunity for this rebellion. Boudicca apparently countenanced barbarous human sacrifice to be performed in the grove of the goddess Andraste, in the flush of rebel success, which shows that she was not averse to the most repellent feature of Druidical practice. In an unimportant way the Druids did survive on the continent. They are never heard of again, by this name, in Britain. But worship of the native gods continued without them and their practices.

If Boudicca was inflamed by an attack on the Druids, she was equally ill-disposed to a religious cult which the Romans introduced to the new province, the worship of the Emperor Claudius himself. Emperor-worship was widely practised throughout the empire by the time of the conquest of Britain. The opportunity was taken here to substitute for the annual gatherings of the tribes supervised by the Druids, a gathering to worship the emperor, as a means of inculcating loyalty. This had worked well in Gaul, and in Britain where most tribes had contributed to the Druidical centre on *Mona*, it was hoped that

137

The Temple of Claudius at Colchester

they would be willing to change their affections. But the honour of being high priest was expensive, and probably unpopular. In the new *colonia* at Colchester was erected a massive temple in the classical style, adorned with imported stone for which the British had to pay, unquestionably. In the inner *cella* was the statue of the god, the Emperor Claudius. Boudicca and her rebels regarded this as 'the citadel of everlasting domination', but when passions died away, the Britons no doubt were able to look on emperor-worship in its true light. It did not become a burning issue again until the growth of Christianity led anti-Christians to seize on it as an acid test by which Christians could be identified. Apart from this and smaller officially sponsored centres, altars and temples were set up to, or in honour of, emperors and their divine family all over the province by private individuals. A lead was taken by the King Governor, Cogidubnus, who inspired the erection of a temple to Minerva and Neptune 'in honour of the divine imperial family'. Dedications of this kind have been found from all periods of Roman Britain.

Although the old state religion of Rome, based on Jupiter,

Juno and Minerva, declined in importance under the empire, they were worshipped in the traditional way by Roman citizens in the provinces, which meant the four *coloniae* and perhaps St Albans, and, after the Edict of Caracalla, all free inhabitants of the province.

Another side of official religion was the army's programme of religious ceremonies, some—an ever increasing number—in honour of emperors and their families, past and present, others revivals of the local cults of the earliest days of the city of Rome, as a reminder of the Roman, and Italian, character of the army. A whole series of altars have been found from the parade grounds outside the army's forts in Britain, set up on 3 January each year to Jupiter the Best and Greatest, the traditional chief god of Rome. Each year the commanding officer dedicated a new altar, and the old one was buried, in annual renewal of the army's allegiance to Rome's protecting deity. In the centre of the headquarters building of the forts, in the *sacellum* (shrine), were housed the standards of the units which the soldiers revered, together with the guardian spirit of the emperors, or the Discipline of the emperors. The shrines of the legionary headquarters, as they were those of citizen units, included altars to Jupiter as well. A host of other spirits protected the commandant's house (*genius praetorii*), the barrack block (*genius centuriae*), the stables (Epona), and the fort bath houses (Fortuna).

In the settlements outside the forts there usually grew up a

Soldiers leading animals to sacrifice

temple quarter, and the same seems to have been the case with the towns. Many of the temples were dedicated to deities imported from other parts of the empire, or from beyond the empire. In London, there was a temple of Isis, the Egyptian goddess, and the Egyptian god Serapis had a temple set up to him at York at the beginning of the third century by the commander of the Sixth Legion, Claudius Hieronymianus, whose name reveals his eastern origin. Another eastern god much worshipped was Jupiter Dolichenus, an identification of the Baal of Doliche with the Roman Jupiter. Dolichenus seems to have had a proselytising priesthood, as many of the dedications are recorded as having been set up 'by command of the god'. At Corbridge, the military town near Hadrian's Wall, two altars were set up in Greek, one to the goddess Astarte (Ashtaroth, 'the abomination of the Sidonians' of the Old Testament), by a certain Pulcher, and the other to Hercules of Tyre, by 'Diodora the high priestess'. Diodora no doubt looked for new devotees among the superstitious soldiers. At Housesteads, the First Cohort of Tungrians set up a corporate dedication 'to the gods and goddesses, according to the interpretation of the oracle of Apollo of Clarus', apparently in response to an imperial order to all army units at this time.

At Carvoran (*Banna*), the First Cohort of Hamii dedicated to the Syrian Goddess, their national deity, and M. Caecilius Donatianus, commanding the same unit, composed an elegant little poem in honour of his own national deity, the African goddess Caelestis (the Carthaginian Tanit), whom he identified with the goddess worshipped by his men. It was not only the easterners in Britain who remembered their national gods. Deities with extraordinary names like Harimella, Ricagambeda, Viradecthis, Garmangabis and the Alaisiagae were worshipped by men from the Rhineland and Germany, to remind them of their homeland. Popular too was the worship of the Mother Goddesses, who are depicted in simple stone reliefs as a group of three female figures, with bowls on their laps symbolising plenty. These goddesses were worshipped in much of the north-western part of the empire, as also was another group, depicted in a relief found at Housesteads, the *Genii Cucullati*—

'hooded spirits'—wearing the hooded cloaks favoured by inhabitants of that part of the empire.

One of the most powerful religions of the empire, Mithraism, found a footing in Britain as well as other provinces. Originally a Persian god, Mithras was being worshipped by Romans by the first century B.C., and

The 'hooded spirits'

in succeeding centuries his influence increased. Mithraic ritual was hallowed by a complex mythology in which the highest god of all was Aeon, 'boundless time', represented as a lion-headed monster whose body was encircled by a snake, the sinuous folds of which symbolised the tortuous ecliptic course of the sun. Beneath Aeon were the gods of light and darkness, the beneficent Ahura Mazda and the evil Ahriman. Mithras was thought of as an intermediary, the mediator between gods and men. In the Mithraic legend, the young Mithras had captured a wild bull which the Raven, messenger of the sun, ordered him to slay. From the blood of the bull sprang up life-giving vegetation, and from the procreative fluid animal life.

A Mithraic ceremony in progress

The scorpion, dog and serpent, instruments of Ahriman, attempted to attack and poison the vital parts of the bull, but Mithras with his two companions defeated their attempts and was thus portrayed as the beneficent provider of good for mankind. He was also closely associated with the sun god, and was often identified with him as 'Mithras, the unconquered sun'. His temples were small secret places (originally he had been worshipped in caves). His great act of redemption, the bull slaying, was generally represented in a painted frieze or sculptured relief which formed a kind of altar piece behind the altars. The god's two companions, bearing torches, Cautes, with torch uplifted, representing life, light, heat and the day, and Cautopautes with torch turned down, representing death, darkness, cold and night, were generally depicted with him.

The worshippers of Mithras formed their own priesthood, being initiated before they could participate in the ceremonies of the cult. They could then rise gradually through seven grades,

Mithras, the bull-slayer

about which little is known for certain, except their names, such as Soldier, Raven, Lion and Father. In the temple was a coffin-like ritual pit, in which at some stage the initiate had to lie in darkness, although it is clear that he was not washed in bull's blood, as is sometimes thought. In Britain the traces of Mithraic worship have been found mainly in the military zone of the north, and in London, which is not surprising as the qualities of truthfulness and fortitude required of the initiates were especially admired by soldiers and by merchants, and this exotic cult, restricted to men only, had little appeal to the peasants and townsmen of the rest of the province. At

Head of Mithras from London

the end of the second century the Emperor Commodus was himself initiated. In the third century the ritual bull slaying appeared on a medallion of Gordian III, and at the end of this century the emperor Aurelian established the worship of 'the unconquered sun' as a new official religion. In 308, the emperors Diocletian, Maximian, Galerius and Licinius, meeting at *Carnuntum*, the great military headquarters on the Danube near Vienna, dedicated an altar to Mithras, as 'the supporter of their empire'. But at this moment Constantine the Great had already begun his attempt to gain sole rule, which was to end in success for himself and official recognition for Christianity. The temple of Mithras at Carrawburgh (*Brocolitia*) on the Wall seems to have been deliberately destroyed in the fourth century, perhaps by Christians, and that in London (the Walbrook Mithraeum) seems likewise to have met opposition which impelled its worshippers to conceal the sculptures which adorned it.

Christianity and Mithraism were in fact never true rivals. Mithraism was far more exclusive, with its restriction to men, and its emphasis on military qualities. Christian writers speak of Mithraism as a rival, with loathing and contempt, and

Constantine, the first Christian emperor

certainly many aspects of the cult resembled their own, not only the person of Mithras as a redeemer and mediator, but the ritual feast resembling the Eucharist, and the initiation ceremonies reminiscent of baptism. But its devotees were always drawn from a smaller class than those of Christianity. The dedicants of the altars in the Carrawburgh Mithraeum were all commanding officers of the Cohort of Batavians stationed there; men of rank from Italy and the western provinces. In London, the devotees were wealthy merchants, and one at least a legionary veteran. The temples were small and could not hold more than a dozen worshippers at one time. At one end was the sanctuary, with the altars and bull-slaying altar piece, facing which was a narrow nave lined with benches. A kind of ante-chapel was screened off at the other end, where there was a hearth on which the incense of pine cones could be burned and the ordeal pit in which the ritual initiation took place.

Although Constantine the Great began his victorious career with his proclamation as emperor by the army at York in 306, after the death of his father Constantius Chlorus, there is little evidence that Christianity, the religion which he was to establish, was widespread in Britain at this time. The Christian writer Tertullian, a century before, had claimed that 'places of the Britons inaccessible to the Romans' had been imbued with the faith, meaning presumably Scotland or even Ireland, but he himself lived in North Africa, and there is little evidence to support this claim. Britain's first Christian martyr Alban probably met his end at *Verulamium* in the persecution under Diocletian at the beginning of the fourth century. After the protection of Christianity by Constantine, the British church came into the light of day with its fellow churches, and in 314, three British bishops, Eborius of York, Restitutus of London, and Adelphius of Lincoln, accompanied by Sacerdos an elder and

144

Arminius a deacon, who may have represented a fourth bishop unable to be there, attended the church council at Arles. In 359, three British bishops were present at Rimini who were so poor that their expenses had to be paid for them, which has suggested that their dioceses were neither large nor prosperous, but in fact probably indicates that they firmly adhered to the rules of personal poverty of the primitive church.

Even so, it is clear that Christianity was slow to flourish in Britain, as was natural in a province further than any other from the homeland of the faith. The legends of Joseph of Arimathea and the Holy Grail, and of visits by various apostles, cannot be proved or disproved, but are unlikely to be true. It is more convincing to hear of British Christianity in connection with the martyrdom of Alban. The reasons which motivated the Roman government to persecute Christianity in the days before Constantine were originally political. Purely formal worship of the official gods was a sign of Roman patriotism to which increasing importance was attached as the empire ran into difficulties in the third century. The Christians refused to conform, and at first it was official policy to ignore them unless they were publicly accused, in which case they were tried before a magistrate, given the opportunity of conforming, and, if they refused, executed. The actual numbers martyred in this way were small, but many found the Christians a convenient scapegoat to allay popular discontent at a time when plague, famine, civil war and external attack appeared to endanger the very existence of an empire which it had been prophesied would last for ever. The Christians were blamed as atheists, who by ignoring, or despising, the ancestral gods had provoked their wrath. Constantine had the insight to see in the Christians a rejuvenating spiritual force for a tottering empire. In the eyes of some, such as Edward Gibbon, he thereby hastened its downfall.

The Lullingstone Christian

Official recognition of Christianity did not mean the immediate abandonment of pagan cults. Indeed, in Britain the reverse

145

seems to have been the case. There was a revival of pagan practices under the threat of licensed competition. The Christians did undoubtedly destroy many pagan temples, but pagans were ready to restore them. The beautiful silver dish, known as the Corbridge Lanx, was probably the possession of a wealthy man who admired the Emperor Julian's pro-pagan policy, for it depicts a scene directly inspired by his revival of the cult of Apollo at Delos, during his brief reign in the mid fourth century. Another pagan cult which particularly flourished in the fourth century was that of the god Nodens at Lydney on the Severn. Nodens was a god of hunting and a water god, who had also healing powers. On a hill top above the Severn estuary was built a large temple with nave and side chapels in the surrounding court, which was adorned with expensive mosaic pavements, one of them paid for by the commandant of a naval repair yard (*praefectus reliquationis*) and his interpreter, who visited the site.

The Corbridge Lanx

As well as the temple, there was a large guest house for pilgrims, built around a central court, baths, and a long portico divided into cells, in which it is thought the pilgrims would seek healing. The design of the place as a religious centre is most unusual and seems clearly influenced by

Senecianus' ring from Silchester

Christian monasticism. There is indeed a hint that the worshippers of Nodens and Christ clashed directly on one occasion. A ring has been found at Silchester bearing the inscription 'Senecianus, may you live in God', a formula of Christian type. Senecianus had not been the first owner of the ring, for the name of Venus, pagan goddess of love was inscribed underneath. At Lydney a certain Silvianus dedicated to Nodens, having lost a ring which Nodens as a god of hunting should have been able to help him to find, and promised to pay half its value to the god if successful, recording also his suspicion that a certain Senecianus had stolen it. It would be a coincidence if the ring of Silvianus were the one found at Silchester, in which case his suspicions of Senecianus were fully justified.

Worshippers of the pagan gods had a simple relationship with their chosen divinity. They asked for assistance, and, if it seemed to have been granted, they repaid the god with a promised reward, which was either in the form of an altar or a sacrifice. Some deities like Nodens, and Sulis who presided over the hot springs at Bath, were credited with healing powers as well. Mostly the grateful dedicators of altars left no details of what their god had done for them, simply the formula 'v.s.l.m.' (*Votum solvit libens merito*, 'willingly performs his vow which was deserved'). Further details such as those given by Silvianus when making his vow, or the boastful thanks for his hunting prowess of Veturius Micianus the cavalry colonel, are not often found.

Many of the deities worshipped in Roman Britain were personifications, in the Roman manner, of the Celtic nature

147

North Tyne river god

spirits. Where the spirits' names were unknown, the Roman would dedicate to the 'genius, or spirit, of the place' (*genius loci*), or to 'the nymphs and genius of the place'. Sometimes the nymphs did have a name, such as Coventina who presided over a spring outside the fort of Carrawburgh on the Wall, into which generations of worshippers cast coins to gain good luck. Rivers too were personified, such as the Wharfe—*Verbeia*—and were sometimes portrayed as venerable river gods: Old Father Thames or Father North Tyne.

One of the most striking examples of religious dedications is the group of altars found at Auchendavy

Altar of Cocceius Firmus

on the Antonine Wall, which recorded dedications made to as many as twelve different deities. The pious centurion M. Cocceius Firmus, who set them up, was a worshipper of Jupiter, Best and Greatest, Victory the Victorious, Diana and Apollo (who have been explained as Balkan deities with Roman names), of the Spirit of the Land of Britain, of Mars, Minerva, the Campestres, Hercules, Epona, Victory once more, without the epithet 'victorious', and Silvanus. Epona was goddess of horses, and the Campestres were deities with special interest in cavalrymen. The centurion Cocceius Firmus reveals himself by his choice of gods as an ex-cavalryman (more particularly, from the Imperial Horse Guards) of Balkan origin. The altars to Jupiter, Victory, Mars and Minerva are natural for any patriotic Roman. Hercules, the hero deified for his labours, and Silvanus the god of hunting are

148

not surprising, nor indeed is the Spirit of the Land of Britain. The Romans happily personified regions, rivers, or springs and worshipped them in full accordance with Celtic feeling. Dedications have been found too to Brigantia, the patron goddess of the great Pennine confederation, including a startling relief showing her as a war goddess.

It was very common for the Romans or natives alike to give the local gods a twin name. Thus Sulis the goddess of the Bath springs became Sulis Minerva. Cocidius, the Cumbrian god, was sometimes identified with Mars, god of war, and sometimes with Silvanus, god of the woodland and of hunting. Maponus, whose worship was centred a little north of Hadrian's Wall, was identified with Apollo, which means presumably that his cult was one connected with peaceful festivals. Often the names were confused, in particular that of a mysterious northern

A dedication to the goddess Brigantia

deity called sometimes Huitris, sometimes Vitiris, and sometimes in the plural, the *Di Veteres*—'the old gods'—a name suggesting that the deity was worshipped by militant anti-Christian pagans in this last guise. It is interesting to notice a class distinction among votaries of the gods. Apollo Maponus and Mars Cocidius were worshipped by men of standing. Mars Belatucadrus and Huitris or Vitiris were worshipped by the lower classes, to judge from the character of dedications.

The temples in which these deities were worshipped varied greatly, but most were of one standard design, known as Romano-Celtic, in which a square *cella*, or inner shrine, was surrounded by a square outer wall, enclosing the *temenos*, or sacred precinct. A few temples only, such as that of Claudius at Colchester and of Sulis Minerva at Bath, were built in

Head of the Gorgon from the Temple of Sulis Minerva at Bath

the full classical style, with columns, podium and pediment. A great number of Romano-Celtic temples have been found, varying only in size and lavishness of ornamentation. Smaller shrines were sometimes round or octagonal, such as the temple of Mars Thincsus and the Alaisiagae set up in the *vicus* of the fort at Housesteads by German mercenaries, which was a crudely constructed circular building 13 feet in diameter, built without foundations over a ruined cobbler's shop. Temples of Mithras and Christian churches had their own design, dictated by the nature of their ceremonies. The typical gods of Roman Britain were not worshipped corporately, but in private, singly. Occasional exceptions are found where the temples seem to have been associated with a fair, such as at Pagans Hill in Somerset and Gosbecks near Colchester. There games and festivals seem to have been held, perhaps in connection with the fertility rites designed to make the land and livestock give of their best in the season to come.

It was in the end Christianity which was successful. Its traces in Britain, once very scanty, have in recent years become much clearer and more convincing. At many different places all over the country small scattered relics, Christian symbols such as the Chi-Rho, and a few tombstones with Christian formulas, have been found. Flavius Antigonus Papias, who was buried at Carlisle, had his age put on his tombstone, not with the exactitude which pagans thought essential, but with the words '*plus minus*' —more or less—and Brigomaglos was buried outside the fort of *Vindolanda* with the formula '*hic iacit*', but he perhaps belongs to the fifth century. The inscription *Vivas in Deo,* 'may you live in God', and other such Christian mottoes, on cups or jars, are another indication. A building was excavated at Silchester which seems to have been a church, although the evidence is not conclusive. But at Lullingstone villa in the fourth century, the rich landowners had a Christian chapel adorned with wall paintings (p. 145). Bede mentions that Augustine was able to use a church in Canterbury founded in Roman times, and there must in fact have been a number of churches all over the country. The mosaic of the beardless Christ at Hinton St Mary in Dorset is only the most dramatic of several recent discoveries which lend backing to this assertion. At the very end of the Roman period, two Britons who became well known beyond the province come into view. The first was Pelagius, the famous heretical writer attacked by Augustine, and the second was Patrick, the apostle of Ireland. In the fifth century, after the Roman garrison and Roman tax collectors had gone, the province maintained its connection with the Christian church. For a time the heresy of Pelagius held sway, but two visits by Bishop Germanus (St Germain) were able to eradicate it.

Further Reading

C. M. Daniels, *Mithras and his Temples on the Wall*, 1962 (obtainable from the Joint Museum of Antiquities, Newcastle-upon-Tyne)

W. F. Grimes, 'Recent Excavations in the City of London', in R. L. S. Bruce-Mitford (ed.), *Recent Archaeological Excavations in Great Britain*, 1956

M. J. T. Lewis, *Temples in Roman Britain*, 1966

T. G. E. Powell, *The Celts* (2nd ed.), 1959: Chapter 3, 'The Celtic Supernatural'

I. A. Richmond, 'The Cult of Mithras and its Temple at Carrawburgh' in Bruce-Mitford, *op. cit.*

I. A. Richmond, *Roman Britain* (2nd ed.), 1963: Chapter Five, 'Religious Cults'

Anne Ross, *Pagan Celtic Britain*, 1967

IX

Romans or Britons

The Emperor Hadrian, according to his biographer, built the Wall which bears his name 'to separate the Romans and the barbarians'. By the time of Hadrian many changes had taken place in the island which had made it more Roman in its outward and visible appearance, and Hadrian himself was to give active encouragement to this process of Romanisation, notably to the urban communities. By building the Wall, he set a limit (albeit one that was soon, for a time, disregarded) to the boundaries of the province, and determined that the provincials, those who lived to the south of the Wall, should become Roman rather than barbarian. Certainly, the Emperor Antoninus Caracalla (who reigned as sole emperor, 212–17) made all the Britons, as well as all other free inhabitants of the empire, full Roman citizens in name and legal status. From an early stage, after the invasion of 43, individual Britons had been rewarded with the citizenship, not only native potentates like Cogidubnus, King and Deputy of the Emperor, but men like the father of Claudia Rufina. This lady, whose name Claudia demonstrates that the family's citizenship was obtained from Claudius or Nero, lived in the latter part of the first century in or near Rome, where she was married to a friend of the poet Martial, who immortalised her:

> *Though brought up among the sky-blue Britons*
> *She has the spirit of the Latin race.*

The southern Britons, at any rate, had given up the use of blue woad even before the Roman conquest, but the blueness of Britons continued to be a stock epithet, later transferred to the Picts. The 'spirit of the Latin race' was perhaps never acquired to the full by the Roman Britons, but by the last years of Roman Britain, many aspects of life in the province had become as fully Roman as in Italy or the western provinces. Rome itself had changed much in the centuries during which Britain was a province of the empire, and it is questionable whether Martial

Hadrian, Emperor 117–38

would have found the old Latin spirit in the Italy of the early fifth century. But it is worth remembering that Martial himself, and the emperor Hadrian, were both provincial Romans from Spain, and while no doubt largely of Italian colonial stock, very probably had some native Spanish blood as well.

But it is not simply a question of contrast between Roman and Briton; the Roman world was a polyglot, cosmopolitan world, with freedom of movement for civilians, and a great deal of movement for people in the administration or in the armed forces. Second-century governors of Britain, for example, can be shown to have come from Africa, Spain, Cilicia (in modern Turkey) and Dalmatia (in modern Yugoslavia) as well as from Italy; and one legionary commander, A. Claudius Charax, was a Greek-speaking historian from Pergamum in the west of Asia Minor. The equestrian officers were drawn from an even wider number of regions, Gaul and the Rhineland, the Danubian provinces, Egypt and the eastern provinces, as well as the areas already mentioned. If the centurionate and the other ranks in the legions and auxiliary regiments are included, the picture is of a hotch-potch from the entire empire. Many of the veteran soldiers clearly settled in Britain on their discharge, as the finds of their discharge certificates (*diplomata*) indicate. It is doubtful whether the population of the country has ever been more cosmopolitan than it was in the Roman period. The case of the Palmyrene trader Barates has been mentioned already in an earlier chapter; the fact that he added to the tombstone of his British wife an inscription in his native language and script, and that the funeral relief was carved in the style of the homeland, implies that there was a Palmyrene community at South Shields, just as there is an Arab community there today. But there was a complete absence of racial feeling in the Roman empire, and inter-marriage called for no comment. Admittedly, the number of inscriptions relating to civilians from other parts of the empire is not large, but it is worth noting the presence of a Greek buried at Carlisle, a boy with a Semitic name buried by his father in Scotland in the second century, the young Hermes from Commagene in Asia Minor buried at Brough under Stainmore, and the woman from Dalmatia, whose soldier husband buried her at Carvoran early in the third century. All these examples are from the military zone. In the south of the province, particularly in London, the exotic element in the population would be even higher.

Britain, which had been a kind of El Dorado to imaginative Romans before the conquest, before long lost its curiosity value, and Roman interest in the province became predominantly military for most of its history. Britain was an important source of man-power for the imperial armies, and for its first 150 years as a province was one of the senior appointments for a senator with military ambitions. Through this chance, much of the early history of the Roman occupation is known from the pages of Tacitus' *Agricola*. The later history of the province is in many places obscure, and even at the end of the fourth century, a few years before the year 410, when the Roman government sundered its links with the administration and defence of the province, the comparatively large number of references in the poems of the court poet Claudian do not cast much light on the course of events:

> *The Saxons are defeated and the sea is safe;*
> *Britain is delivered with the overthrow of the Picts.*

In general, Britain was clearly regarded as the most remote of all provinces, and was perhaps even the Roman Siberia for troublemakers, both political and religious. It is recorded of Marcus Aurelius that in the 170s, when he had to deal with Tiridates, a dissident native ruler in the East, 'Marcus did not put him to death, but merely sent him to Britain'. In the fourth century, a certain Valentinus, exiled to Britain by the Emperor Valentinian, tampered with the loyalty of the troops there and plotted a rebellion. Later in the fourth century, a number of supporters of the Priscillianist heresy were sent into exile on the Scilly Isles.

Britain's positive contribution to the public life of the empire seems to have been small. No army officer of British origin above the rank of chief centurion is known, and only one man of equestrian rank, a certain Macrinius from Colchester, who is not known to have served in the army or administration in any case. But M. Macrinius Vindex, commander of the imperial Guard in the reign of Marcus Aurelius, and his relative, the brilliant senatorial general M. Macrinius Avitus Catonius Vindex, were enrolled in the same voting district as was, probably, Colchester, and the name Macrinius is a typical Latinisation of an original Celtic name. So these two distinguished men, and others like them, could well be of British origin. Certainly, in the fourth century, Britons were playing an active role in the forefront of affairs; men such as the usurper Magnentius (half British, as was the third-century usurper Bonosus, son of a British schoolmaster); and in the first decade of the fifth century the British army set up three pretenders to the throne in succession, the third of whom, known as Constantine III, ruled for several years over the three major western provinces, and for a time was within sight of controlling the whole of the western empire.

In the preceding chapters something has been said about the way in which the material life of the inhabitants of Britain

Magnentius, a usurper of British origin

Aylesford bucket handle

was influenced by Rome, and in the chapter devoted to religion it has been pointed out how the native and imported cults were able to live side by side. One field so far mentioned only in passing deserves a fuller treatment, the effect on artistic life. In this field the effect of Rome was not really for the better. As in many cases where a higher civilisation is imposed, the vigorous expression of native artists was inhibited by Roman artistic standards, and the attempts to imitate Roman art produced something inferior to the native product. The Celtic peoples of Britain had a flourishing artistic style of high merit at the time of the Roman conquest. It was an offshoot of the Celtic art of the Continent, known, after one of its chief centres, as La Tène art. The Celts were attracted above all by abstract designs and a love of curving, spiral form. In portraying human or animal forms they made no attempt to achieve the exact realism of classical Mediterranean art. A good example of the Celtic style of the pre-Roman period can be seen in the head which decorates a bucket handle found at Aylesford. The great staring eyeballs, geometrically stylised nose and gaunt, hollow cheeks produce a powerful overall effect, very different from a realistic classical portrait. The Aylesford head, with its grotesque and elaborate helmet, gives a terrifying effect of the supernatural, a kind of formal religious distortion of the human face.

Stylisation: wild boar from Hounslow

Naturally, influences from the Continent were already making themselves felt before the Roman conquest. A striking example of their effect can be seen by comparing two figures of wild boars made by British artists. The first, found at Hounslow, is a splendid example of the developed Celtic style. The animal's form is distorted, but the economical stylisation has produced something alive and menacing. The bold way in which the bristles of the spine are rendered as a mere half dozen crests, and the sullen snout and ears, give a splendid overall effect. By contrast, a wild boar of bronze found at Lexden, made about A.D. 1, is completely naturalistic. The head and body are quite life-like, and the spine-bristles

Naturalism: boar from Lexden

have been carefully engraved. The result is that the animal looks almost tame in comparison with the fierce creature from Hounslow.

The Celtic love of spiral form could be illustrated by many examples. A bronze-plated iron spearhead found in the Thames illustrates one particular aspect of this love of spiral form particularly well, for the curving decorative scroll is asymmetrical: the weapon itself was perfectly symmetrical, but the four pieces of decoration are all of different shapes, which nevertheless produce a satisfying harmony of style. But in this sphere, too, the influence of Roman styles across the Channel had some effect. The mirror from Desborough, for example, with its swelling, trumpet-like curves, although a superb piece

Bronze-plated iron spearhead, showing Celtic love of asymmetrical decoration

The Desborough mirror

of dynamic drawing, somehow has lost the rhythmic movement of the pure Celtic style, because the two halves of the flowing pattern are exactly symmetrical.

The advent of the Romans meant that the province was rapidly flooded with mass produced articles of Roman manufacture, notably Samian pottery, which, although in its early days of quite high artistic merit, soon degenerated into something dull and stereotyped. Sculpture was not produced in the official Roman manner. Many of the sculptures of the Roman period found in Britain were naturally imported, and are of standard classical type. But it is often possible to detect examples which have been carved by native craftsmen unhappy with the new realistic style, although the head of the Gorgon from the temple of Sulis Minerva at Bath depicting a theme of classical origin in a realistic manner (p. 150), is regarded as a successful and impressive harmonising of Roman and Celtic art. Sometimes, the compromise was a happy one, resulting in a work of merit. The head of the native god Antenociticus, for example, from Benwell (*Condercum*) on Hadrian's Wall, has the serenity and detailed accuracy of classical models, but the native artist has somehow infused his work with a Celtic otherworldliness, notably in the geometrical way in which the hair is arranged.

The native god Antenociticus

To a certain extent the native style survived, particularly in the more primitive zone of the province. A notable example is the tombstone of a child called Pervica, from Greatchesters (*Aesica*) on the Wall, which makes no more than a formal condescension to the traditional Roman form of tombstone. It treats the subject in very low relief, making it no more than a silhouette, and ignores the details of dress and portraiture which the Roman carvers sought faithfully to render. The result is what has been called 'a barbaric abstraction', which has occasioned the surmise that 'a superstitious fear of the likeness as an abode for the ghost produced this astonishing exercise in abstract art' (T. D. Kendrick). Another fine piece of traditional native art, found at the same place as Pervica's

Tombstone of Pervica, Greatchesters

tombstone, is the Aesica brooch, decorated in true Celtic manner with embossed scrolls of spiral form.

Another good example of the way the native art was able to survive is provided by Castor-ware pottery. Significantly, decoration on Castor pots was applied individually, by the barbotine method, unlike the Samian ware which it largely replaced. Thus the skills and tastes of the individual potters could play a fuller role. The favourite form of decoration was of hunting scenes, with dogs chasing hares round the bowl (p. 128). The fantastically elongated form of the animals is in the true Celtic tradition, with the favoured spiral forms reappearing in the shape of leaves. When the Castor potters tried to portray a huntsman as well, the result was less happy, and when they

The Aesica brooch

Castor-ware pot

tried a typical classical theme, such as gladiators fighting, or Hercules rescuing Hesione, the result was stereotyped and even absurd.

In the end, the Celtic style survived, and was to reappear in the fifth and succeeding centuries. Ultimately, with new vigour given from Ireland, it was to have a powerful effect on early Anglo-Saxon art, notably in the great Northumbrian illuminated manuscript, written about 700, known as the Lindisfarne Gospels. But throughout the Roman period the Roman style dominated. Not only in the towns and elegant country houses, but in peasants' cottages and hovels, the mass produced products of the empire were present, almost obliterating the native style.

Although Roman material civilisation dominated, it is difficult to be certain to what extent the Latin language and the Latin spirit permeated British society. It would, indeed, hardly be expected that Claudia Rufina, the elegant and refined Roman British lady admired by Martial, was not an exception to the rest of her countrymen and countrywomen. Agricola is said to have succeeded in making the adoption of Roman dress popular, for example, but this was probably confined to the upper classes, and there is little evidence for the extent to which the toga was worn. Certainly the British peasants continued to wear the hooded cloak. The British monk Gildas, writing in the sixth century, refers to Latin as 'our language'. But in most of Britain the language of the Anglo-Saxon invaders dominated, and where it did not, Celtic, not Latin, survived. It is true that the area where Celtic survived was precisely the least civilised part of the former province, and that to a certain extent the use of Anglo-Saxon may have replaced Latin rather than Celtic in the lowland part of Britain. But there is an interesting fact about the Latin that was spoken in Britain. Apparently it was Latin of the purest and most classical kind, indicating that it was the speech of the upper classes, rather than of the common people. In other provinces, the vulgar Latin used by the common people became a *lingua franca* for all classes in society. Of course Latin left its mark on Welsh where hundreds of words are derived from Latin originals, and even Anglo-Saxon incorporated a few Latin words, such as *strata*, becoming 'street'.

A significant commentary on the extent to which Latin was used is provided by *graffiti*—words or remarks scratched on tiles or pieces of pottery. Nearly half of these have been found in the towns, another two-fifths at military sites, and only a tiny proportion—less than a fifth—in the countryside, most of which are, in any case, cases where a man's name has been scratched on a dish or cup. In London, not surprisingly, a profusion of writing implements has been found, in villas hardly any. Significant also is the fact that three-quarters of all the *graffiti* were scratched on Samian, which suggests that it was the better-off class which was also the literate class. The absence of any inscriptions or *graffiti* in Celtic is an indication that only Latin speakers were literate.

Although Tacitus records that his father-in-law as governor made arrangements for the sons of leading men in Britain to be instructed in the liberal arts and that he himself expressed a preference for the talents of the Britons over those of the Gauls, little evidence has survived of the fruits of this eloquence. Apart from Christian writers, such as Patrick and Pelagius, we know of only one British writer, a poet named Silvius Bonus (whose works have not survived). In fact, Bonus is only known because the Gallic nobleman and writer, Ausonius, wrote a satirical poem on his name: Bonus (meaning 'good') was, according to Ausonius, an impossible name for a Briton, as a good Briton was a contradiction in terms.

Two Britons known to us from the closing years of the country's history as a province of the empire provide a good contrast. Patrick, kidnapped at the age of 16, was not fluent in Latin by that age, although his father and grandfather had been in holy orders and his father had been a magistrate (or possibly an army officer). Patrick apologises in his writings for his lack of education and his 'rustic, unleavened style'. His excuse was that he had to change from the 'language of childhood into an alien tongue', that is, from Celtic to Latin. By contrast, Pelagius, the famous (or notorious) British heretic, a leading intellectual opponent of Augustine, had received a full education in the classical authors, as well as in later Christian writers. There is no evidence that he left Britain before he reached manhood, and he very probably could have received a good school education at home. But no university is known to have existed in Britain such as those in Gaul at Autun and Bordeaux, with professorships endowed by the government. Pelagius is the first male inhabitant of Britain of whose appearance we possess a description. (Boudicca, several centuries before, had been painted in lavish colours by Roman historians, though how accurately we cannot say.) As a heretic, he was naturally portrayed in unsympathetic fashion by men like Augustine who were at pains to discredit the doctrines he upheld. He is described at one time as a British snake, at others as a mountain dog, through which the devil barked. He was said to be bull-necked, full of face and stern of brow, broad-shouldered like a wrestler, corpulent and slow-moving like a tortoise, weighed down with Scottish porridge, reared on baths and banquets, and even like a Goliath. In spite of these insults, it is possible to gain a fairly coherent picture of the man's appearance. Aside from this, however, it is difficult to believe that Pelagius was a completely exceptional Briton; by the fourth century at any rate, there must have been a reasonable number of highly educated Britons. Even in the fifth century there were enough men who cared about the finer points of theological doctrines to be supporters of the Pelagian heresy, making it necessary for St Germanus, Bishop of Auxerre, to make two visits to the island in an attempt to stamp the heresy out. But it must be admitted that Pelagius' learning was probably of an unusually high order, for St Augustine, his opponent, conceded that Pelagius was so much better educated than himself in Greek, that he felt at a disadvantage when opposing him before a Greek-speaking audience.

The evidence from the towns suggests that literacy and

knowledge of Latin was widespread among all urban classes. Certainly the artisan class knew enough Latin to scratch on an unbaked tile remarks such as 'Clementinus made this box-tile' (*fecit tubul. Clementinus*), a date in the Roman manner, such as 'six days before the Kalends of October', or just *satis*— 'enough'. Other tiles have indications of more interesting comments such as one where the only word left is *puellam*— 'girl', and another one (already mentioned in Chapter VI) which looks like part of a writing lesson, and ends up with a quotation from Virgil—*conticuere omnes*. If and when other towns are excavated as fully as Silchester where these examples were found, similar evidence will no doubt be forthcoming. The Virgilian tag is especially interesting, as Virgilian themes were popular in designs of mosaics. At Lullingstone there is even an elegiac couplet referring to the *Aeneid*. It is interesting that the only quotation from Virgil which appeared on the Roman coinage was on the coinage of the 'British emperor', the usurper Carausius, one of whose coins carried the legend *expectate veni*—'come, thou long awaited'. Carausius or his mint-master must have expected at least some of his subjects who used his coinage to appreciate the learned reference.

When Britain was restored to the control of the central government it fell under the immediate rule of Constantius Chlorus, the western Caesar (junior emperor), who commemorated the occasion with a medallion struck at Trier, depicting on the reverse the arrival of Constantius at London. The Emperor, on horseback, is greeted by the personified city of London kneeling before him outside the city walls. The legend inscribed on the medallion is revealing of official thought: *redditor lucis aeternae*— 'restorer of the eternal

Lullingstone mosaic, with lines recalling Virgil

Constantius arrives at London

light'. Thus the return of the province to full participation in the empire is proclaimed to be a return to the civilising values of Rome. In view of the apparent high intellectual level of the coinage of Carausius, this was perhaps not so significant a change as the propaganda of Constantius claimed. One significant change which began, in a sense, in Britain, and affected the whole empire, and the subsequent history of the world, was that the Roman army of Britain proclaimed Constantine as emperor when his father Constantius died at York in 306. Constantine began in Britain his path to supreme power which resulted in freedom of worship for the first time for the persecuted Christians—but also profoundly changed the character of the empire.

A pleasant illustration of the meaning of Rome to the British provincials is provided by a mosaic pavement from Aldborough in the North Riding of Yorkshire. Aldborough (*Isurium Brigantum*) was the chief town of the *civitas* which it had taken the longest time to subdue, much of whose territory remained

Mosaic from Aldborough in Yorkshire

under military government. A wealthy citizen of the Brigantes chose as the subject of the mosaic to adorn a room of his house, the wolf and twins legend—the foundation legend of the city of Rome. The curiously barbaric representation of the wolf with Romulus and Remus epitomises the relationship between the province and the centre of the empire.

There is a profound difference between the nationalistic anti-

164

Roman fervour of early British rebels against Rome, such as Boudicca, and the fervent appeals of the fifth-century Britons for assistance from the central government against external threats. Boudicca, and the two other leading resisters against Roman rule, Caratacus and Calgacus, are portrayed graphically in the pages of Roman historians. It is not clear how truthful are the opinions attributed to them. Caratacus, a captive brought before the victorious Claudius and his court in Italy when the Brigantian Queen Cartimandua's implacability had led to his final capture, is supposed in a proud speech to have commented with ironical surprise that 'the Romans, with such splendour as they possessed should have coveted the poor hovels of the Britons'. Calgacus, the Caledonian chieftain, is made by Tacitus to comment sardonically on Rome's civilising mission: 'they make a desolation and call it "peace"'. Rebellion in Britain continued sporadically into the second half of the second century, but it was by then confined to the hillmen of the Brigantes. The participation of the British legions in rebellion against the central government at later dates was in civil wars, rather than in nationalistic movements.

The Roman invasion of 43 and the Norman invasion of 1066 mark very definite turning points in the history of this country. Even the year 865, when the most powerful Danish army yet seen (the *mikel here*, as the *Anglo-Saxon Chronicle* calls it) invaded and stayed the winter, marks a more definite stage than any single date which can be found to mark a dividing line between Roman Britain and Anglo-Saxon England. There was no 'departure of the Romans', for, as has been made plain, the Britons were as Roman as any inhabitants of the empire in the early fifth century. By the same token, there was no single invasion of Anglo-Saxons which changed the government of the country within a short space of time, as those of Claudius and William of Normandy did. The year 410 is a convenient date, for in that year Britain was seriously ravaged by Saxon pirates, and the *civitates* of the island appealed to Honorius the western emperor for help. At this moment, Constantine III, the usurping Emperor proclaimed in Britain a few years previously, was still in control of most of the western provinces, but he seems to have

The Saxon shore fort at Portchester

withdrawn much of the garrison of the province to serve his own purposes on the continent. One source records that Britain rebelled against Rome at this period, and it may be that the communities of Britain were able to expel the remnants of Constantine III's administration, before appealing for help from Honorius.

But Honorius himself was in grave difficulty throughout the first decade of the fifth century, as his edicts of the years 406–10 indicate, and on 24 August 410 Alaric and the Visigoths entered and plundered the city of Rome. In his reply to the appeal of the British *civitates*, Honorius told them that 'they should see to their own defence'. This seems to mean that the civilian population was exempted from the provisions of the *lex Iulia de vi publica*, by which men were 'forbidden the use of weapons or missiles . . . except for hunting, on journeys, and on voyages'. From this time on, Britain seems to have been ruled by petty princes for the most part, although in some areas the municipalities seem to have continued to govern for a while. The last desperate appeal to Rome, in 446 (recorded by the sixth-century Welsh chronicler, Gildas), fell on deaf ears: 'the barbarians push us into the sea, the sea pushes us back to the barbarians; between these two sorts of death, we are either slaughtered or drowned.'

The enemies of Roman Britain, against whom the Britons now had to struggle alone, had made their first appearance many years before the opening of the fifth century, but it was then that their attacks intensified, and that one group, the Germanic invaders from across the North Sea, began to settle in force, rather than come merely to plunder. Saxon pirates first disturbed the province towards the end of the third century. At the beginning of the fourth century, Constantius Chlorus had to campaign against the Picts, who appeared under this name for the first time then, although it is clear that under a variety of other names they had been a menace to the northern frontier for some time before that. In the fourth century the Scotti of Ireland began to threaten the west coast of Britain. A climax was reached in the year 367, when Britain was attacked simultaneously by these three peoples, together with the Attacotti and the Franks, in an attack of such magnitude that its origin was ascribed by a Roman historian of the time to a 'barbarian conspiracy'. But the Picts and the Scots never acquired a permanent foothold within the territories of the province, apart from a minor Scottish settlement in western Wales. It was the Germanic peoples who finally took away the Romano-Celtic character from that part of Roman Britain which became England.

It is clear that in spite of the references to the 'arrival

Saxon shore forts in the south-east

Pictish warriors

of the Saxons' (*adventus Saxonum*) in some of the sources, an event which it is difficult to date whatever it is supposed to mean, there was no single moment when the Germanic peoples invaded. It is worth remembering that the Roman government had for a long time been employing barbarian peoples outside the empire as mercenary soldiers. Germans of this kind, such as those commanded by the chieftain Hnaudifridus, were serving on Hadrian's Wall in the early third century. During the third and fourth centuries the process was intensified, and in addition barbarians were given lands as permanent settlers in the province. One example of which the sources speak is that of the Alemanni, some of whom were settled in Britain by the Emperor Valentinian. The names of the chieftains Hengist and Horsa are famous, not to say notorious, in English history. The reason for their arrival is significant: they were summoned to serve as mercenaries by a Roman British ruler named Vortigern, and they stayed and turned against him. Vortigern was behaving in an identical way to the Roman emperors. Indeed, not only soldiers, but high ranking officers of the Roman army were in origin barbarian mercenaries.

In the first part of the fifth century, there are clear indications that Britain was still a Roman island, even if no longer a Roman province. But one piece of evidence is a significant pointer: the last certain date of contact of the Church in Britain with the Continental Church is the year 455, for the changed date of Easter agreed on in that year was adopted by the British Church.

Subsequent changes were not followed in Britain, and the implication is clear that after that date contact had ceased. But the mercenaries brought over by Vortigern established no more than a local ascendancy in south-east England. It was to take several centuries before most of the former province of Britain became England, and even then Wales remained independent.

One of the reasons for this delay was undoubtedly the strength of British resistance, echoes of which can be found in the small historical kernel of truth in the legends of Arthur. Arthur seems to have been a successful general, probably commanding a force of heavy cavalry, and to have been at least partly responsible for checking the Anglo-Saxon advance for at least fifty years. But there were probably many local leaders who performed deeds like those of Arthur. The literary sources tell also of a certain Ambrosius Aurelianus, 'last of the Romans', and of other British generals. One native leader who was clearly responsible for strengthening North Wales against attack (from the west) was Cunedda, King of the Votadini, a people who had occupied the eastern lowlands of Scotland, thus technically outside the Roman province, although the names of his father and grandfather are Roman. He led a force to North Wales where he settled with his people, some time at the beginning of the fifth century. Somehow, most of the deeds of military prowess became attached in popular imagination to a single leader, Arthur the Briton. Even before Geoffrey of Monmouth had for ever distorted the truth with his fictitious *History of the*

Anglo-Saxon warriors

Britons, the fame of Arthur had spread as far as northern Italy, where a sculptured relief portrays Arthur and his knights on an arch of the cathedral at Modena.

Extravagant claims for the influence of Roman rule on the subsequent history of this country must not be made. But it is a matter of doubt whether the Germanic tribes which conquered all but Wales and Scotland would have been tempted to settle in Britain, if its centuries as a Roman province had not made it so luringly attractive to the Saxon: 'Wondrous is this wall-stone; broken by fate, the castles have decayed; the work of giants is crumbling', was the reaction of an Anglo-Saxon poet to the civilisation his people had overthrown. At the same time, the civilisation which the Saxons, Angles, Frisians and other invaders were able to create in Britain reached a higher level than that of their kinsmen whom they left behind in their Continental homeland; and it was no chance that English missionaries such as Wilfrid and Boniface played a significant role in the conversion of the Continental Germans. Again, it is no accident that the Anglo-Saxons were able to create a unified kingdom far sooner than the Continental Germans, and that the kingdoms of the Heptarchy closely followed the political divisions of Roman Britain.

Further Reading

M. P. Charlesworth, *The Lost Province,* 1949
H. P. R. Finberg, *Lucerna,* 1964
Isobel Henderson, *The Picts,* 1967
P. Hunter Blair, *Roman Britain and Early England,* 1963
K. Jackson, *Language and History in Early Britain,* 1953
T. D. Kendrick, *Anglo-Saxon Art,* 1938: Chapters One to Three
Anne Ross, *Pagan Celtic Britain,* 1967
J. M. C. Toynbee, *Art in Roman Britain,* 1962
J. M. C. Toynbee, *Art in Britain Under the Romans,* 1964

Index

The numerals in **heavy type** refer to the pages on which illustrations appear

I. PEOPLE

A. Emperors, Kings, Governors, Procurators, Legionary Legates, etc.

Agricola, *see* Julius
Albinus, *see* Clodius
Allectus, 14, 122
Ambrosius Aurelianus, 169
Antoninus, *see* Caracalla
Arthur, 169, 170
Augustus, 1, 8, 10, 106, 114
Aulus Plautius, *see* Plautius
Aurelian, 121, 143
Aurelianus, *see* Ambrosius
Aurelius, *see* Marcus Aurelius

Bassus, *see* Salvius
Bonosus, 155
Boudicca, 13, 21, 60, 61, 137, 138, 162, 165
Britannicus, 9

Caesar, *see* Julius
Calgacus, 165
Caligula, 8
Caracalla, **39**, 75, 121; Edict of, 23, 47, 48, 68, 139, 152
Caratacus, 8, 9, 31, 165
Carausius, 14, 90, 122, 163, 164
Cartimandua, 165
Catus, *see* Decianus
Classicianus, **21**, 22
Claudius, 8, **9**, 10, 12, **13**, 25, 57, 60, 88, 121, 137, 138, 152, 165
A. Claudius Charax, 153
Ti. Claudius Cogidubnus, 12, 14, 20, 138, 152
Claudius Hieronymianus, 140
Ti. Claudius Paulinus, 18, 19, 24, 131
Clodius Albinus, 21, 56, 90, 127, 130, 131

Cogidubnus, *see* Claudius
Commius, 7, 8
Commodus, 143
Constantine I (the Great), 24, 121, 143, **144**, 164
Constantine III, 26, 155, 165, 166
Constantius I (Chlorus), **14**, 77, 144, 163, **164**, 167
Cunedda, 169
Cunobelinus (Cymbeline), 7–10, 13, 57, 59

Decianus Catus, 78
Diocletian, 121, **122**, 131, 143
Domitian, 115

Falco, *see* Pompeius
Fullofaudes, 48

Galerius, 143
Geta, 39
Gordian III, 143
Gratian, 26

Hadrian, 14, 17, 22, 28, 39, **56**, 63, 74, 77, 106, 152, **153**
Honorius, 12, 165, 166

Julian, 95, 108, 146
Cn. Julius Agricola, 15, 16, 20, 55, 61, 62, 104, 105, 114–116, 160
Julius Caesar, 1, 2, **3**, 4, 6, 7, 10, 57, 82, 123

Licinius, 143

Magnentius, **155**
Magnus Maximus, 26

Marcellus, *see* Neratius, Ulpius, Varius
Marcus, 26
Marcus Aurelius, 24, **25**, 33, 47, 114, 155
Marius Valerianus, 41
Maximian, 143
Maximus, *see* Magnus

Nepos, *see* Platorius
Neratius Marcellus, 18
Nero, 80, 121, 152

Paulinus, *see* Claudius, Suetonius
Pertinax, 55
A. Platorius Nepos, 17, **18**
A. Plautius, 8, 9, 12, 17, 44
Pompeius Falco, 110
Prasutagus, 80
Probus, 126

C. Salvius Liberalis Nonius Bassus, 20
Severus, **14**, 21, 28, 40, 45, 49, 75
Severus Alexander, 41
Stilicho, 48
C. Suetonius Paulinus, 17, 20, 137

Togodumnus, 8, 9

Ulpius Marcellus (1), 55
Ulpius Marcellus (2), 39

Valentinian, 155, 168
Sex. Varius Marcellus, 21, 90
Q. Veranius, 17
Verica, 8
Vespasian, 15, 31, 34
Vortigern, 168, 169

B. Others

Abascantus, *see* Rubrius
Adelphius, bishop, 144
Aelia Matrona, soldier's wife, 46
P. Aelius Magnus, officer, 38
Agrippa, *see* Maenius
Alaric, Goth leader, 166
Alban, martyr, 144, 145
Alexander the Great, 58, 115
Anencletus, slave, 132
Antilochus, charioteer, 73
Appian (qu.), 10

Aristotle (qu.), 58
Arminius, deacon, 145
L. Aruconius Verecundus, businessman, 124
Augustine, St (of Canterbury), 151
Augustine, St (of Hippo), 116, 151
M. Aurelius Lunaris, merchant, 68, 126, 133
M. Aurelius Quirinus, officer, 39, 40

M. Aurelius Salvius, officer, 41
Aurelius Senecio, decurion, 68
Ausonius (qu.), 161
Austalis, workman, 67

Barates, merchant, 133, **134**, 155
Bede (qu.), 161
Bodicca, *see* Lollia
Boniface, missionary, 170
Bonus, *see* Silvius
Brigomaglos, Christian. 150

C. Ancient Peoples, Tribes, etc.

(*See also Places and Subjects, under 'ala' and 'Cohort'*)

II. DEITIES

III. PLACES

IV. SUBJECTS